THE PRACTICE OF SUPERVISING:
Making Experience Pay

SECOND EDITION

MARTIN M. BROADWELL
Training Consultant

ADDISON-WESLEY PUBLISHING COMPANY
Reading, Massachusetts • Menlo Park, California
London • Amsterdam • Don Mills, Ontario • Sydney

Cartoons by Johnny Sajem

Library of Congress Cataloging in Publication Data

Broadwell, Martin M.
    The practice of supervising.

    Includes index.
    1. Supervision of employees. 2. Personnel management.
I. Title.
HF5549.B856   1984   658.3'02   83-21397
ISBN 0-201-10351-6

ISBN: 0-201-10351-6
ABCDEFGHIJ-DO-8987654

To "Aunt Carrie" Broadwell, who wrote her first book at 95

PREFACE TO THE SECOND EDITION

Now there is a second edition! Why? Because we constantly are finding out things we didn't know, thinking of things we didn't say in the first edition, and occasionally discovering things we wish we hadn't said. Our goal is to add more of what we have learned, both in the world of supervising and this author in more experience.

What changes have we made? First, we've been bold enough to suggest that there are some characteristics of good supervisors that are common enough that we can put them down and say that they almost always appear in those we consider as successful supervisors. This suggests that we might have something to imitate if we, too, want to be successful. This will be found in Chapter One. Throughout the book we've stressed the need for and advantage of delegation. In Chapter Six we've pointed out that if we're going to be successful at motivation we're going to have to be successful at *delegation*. A section has been added there just to explain what and to whom we delegate. There is another addition to this chapter on motivation; pointing out that it is not the needs that people have that motivate them to expend energy or do what we want them to do, but rather the *anticipation* of fulfilling that need—an important distinction that is often not made when discussing motivation.

In Chapter Seven we've added some things about how we can better learn the skill of *negotiation*. Not in the sense of employee work agreements, but negotiating agreement between peers, between those who work for us, and even with our bosses. It admits that we don't always see eye-to-eye with others, that we can't always have our way nor give up our desires completely. The solution is to negotiate and this addition should be of help in this direction. In Chapter Eight, we've tried to make discipline "respectable." There is a discussion of why we don't, then some reasons why we end up accepting a guilt-trip from our employees rather than recognizing the good that comes from appropriate discipline.

Finally, in the last chapter, there is an additional aid for those who are interested in furthering their career by knowing themselves better. In fact, we've added some exercises for determining just who we are, what is important to us and what our priorities really are. It tries to help us answer the age-old question: "Who am I?" We invite you to read what's written, give it a chance to work in your life, and if that's good, then we offer congratulations!

Decatur, Georgia   M.M.B.
January 1984

PREFACE TO THE FIRST EDITION

There is a dilemma about supervision. We get the supervisory job because we're moderately capable of handling it. Generally we get little training in the beginning, so we have to learn much on our own. As training is offered, those who are new get first choice, so that the experienced supervisors may again miss a chance to be trained, depending on the cycle of training within the organization. All of this means that we may get off on the wrong foot, develop bad habits, and then miss training that is intended to overcome these deficiencies.

All is not lost, though, for the organization depends upon its experienced supervisors to keep things going while the newer ones get their feet on the ground. It would be presumptuous to suggest that one or two training programs, or even a book or two, can make a person a competent supervisor. Only time, experience, and some agonizingly developed wisdom can do that. It would not be presumptuous, however, to suggest that the backbone of any successful organization is the competency of the experienced supervisors. Those who have struggled with people problems and money and budget problems, and who have gone through the decision-making and problem-solving routines thousands of times, are the ones who keep things rolling. And the fact that not everyone in the organization feels this way, or recognizes it, does not make it less true.

This book is intended to do several things: first, to point out to higher management that the experienced supervisors do play a key role in the organization; second, to show that these experienced supervisors have a right and a need to be kept up to date on the best supervisory practices available; and finally, to give the experienced supervisors a chance to refresh themselves and remind themselves of things they once knew, once practiced, but may have let slip for awhile. It is not complete. It will not make a dramatic change in behavior for the reader. It will serve as a guide in some areas, and a reference in others. To this end is the book dedicated.

Decatur, Georgia   M.M.B.
November 1976

CONTENTS

PROLOGUE

Starting to read a book can be challenging, threatening, or to some exciting. It would be possible for a person to supervise successfully for many years without reading this book. I have no quarrel about that. But it is also possible that the reading of this book might motivate someone to take a long, hard look at himself or herself and decide that there are some things that could be done better than they are now being done. Because the things that are written here come from experience rather than other books, the chances of this are better than average. Let's hope it works for you!

M.M.B.

chapter 1
A LOOK AT SUPERVISION

There are many definitions of the term *supervisor,* and many lists of the supervisor's responsibilities. For the sake of simplicity, let's just say that basically, the supervisor's job is getting work done through other people. Supervisors do many things not directly connected with subordinates, but most of these things are not really the "supervisory" part of the job. People could do them without being called supervisors. Our definition is generally accepted as correct, and gives us the distinctive element we need for the discussions in this book.

THE JOB

The work of a supervisor—getting the job done through other people—is varied. It includes motivating people to work, assigning work for people to do, setting up schedules, planning work, appraising people, counseling employees, solving problems, making decisions, making selections for jobs, setting standards, analyzing jobs, disciplining subordinates, having meetings, going to meetings, communicating, training and developing people, keeping up with organizational goals, and so on. The new supervisor is likely to panic on seeing such a list, wondering how so many skills can be developed in such a short time. Those supervisors who have been around awhile, however, find the list less frightening because they have learned to do these things automatically. The trick, of course, is to learn the skills that are needed for the immediate job, and work on those that will be needed later. But sooner or later, all these skills will be needed. The job of appraising an employee will have to be done some day, whether the skill has been developed or not. Problems are solved every day, and scheduling must be done whether the employee is well trained or not. Promotions are made whether the supervisor is skilled at selection procedures or not. And herein lies one of the bigger problems for the older supervisor: we may get in the habit of doing these things a certain way and, just because the job gets done, assume we're good at it. We then decide that this must be the best way because it's the way we feel most comfortable with. This is the trouble with habit. We feel comfortable with doing things a certain way, so we decide that this way is the ideal because, after all, we must learn to do things in a "natural" way. We confuse "natural" with "habit". Adding to our definition of the supervisor's job, we should point out that the organization has certain goals that need to be reached. Whether or not we have been involved in setting these goals, we are assigned the job of getting the employees under us to work in such a way that these goals are met. The closer we are to the actual production, the more we are inclined to worry less about *how* we do things and more about just *getting them done.* Under these circumstances, the experienced supervisor may fail to develop the proper skills for doing the job well.

WHAT IS GOOD SUPERVISION?

Having defined supervision as getting the job done through other people, we need to decide what good and bad supervision are. Can we say that good supervision is getting a lot of work done? That may be part of it, but is certainly not all there is to it. We can't look at *quantity* alone; we have to look also at *quality.* But quality is sometimes illusive. For example, if we meet a deadline that was difficult to meet, but leave our employees disgruntled, how high was the quality of our supervision? Meeting difficult deadlines is commendable, but creating poor morale is not. Let's take a look at the following case and decide about the matter of good supervision:

Marjorie Adams has been a staff supervisor for nearly ten years. Although she came up through the ranks in the same department where she is now a supervisor, she never worked with any of the people she is presently supervising. The job of Marjorie's group is to see that supplies for the entire department are requisitioned and distributed. Marjorie has no responsibility for controlling the amount of supplies used, since each group must account for its own by signing out the supplies it receives. Monthly inventories are taken of the supplies on hand in Marjorie's storerooms, and matched against purchases and accounting records.

Over the last several years, it has been a matter of pride that Marjorie's inventory records have never had an error. In fact, asked at any time during the month how she stands, Marjorie can give an almost errorless estimation of every item. She has developed an ordering routine that she's very proud of. The people who work for her are trained to the system, and things flow without a hitch, month after month. Special forms—also developed by Marjorie—are used by anyone ordering supplies or taking supplies from the supply room. These forms are then transformed into accounting records, and the information is transferred at the same time to "material to be ordered" forms. It is indeed a smoothly running operation.

Now let's go back to our question of what is good supervision. Is Marjorie Adams a *good* supervisor? If management looks to her to get the kinds of results she is getting, and *no more*, then she is a good supervisor. She meets deadlines, she is creative about the job, she is interested in the job being done as well as possible, and she looks for ways to improve efficiency. All of this is commendable. Furthermore, she keeps good records, she is on top of the job at all times, and she is consistent, getting the same good results month after month. Surely top management would say that Marjorie is a good supervisor. But wait. Let's hear some more about Marjorie. Here is a conversation between Marjorie and her boss during an appraisal session:

"So, Marjorie, I thought we ought to talk a little about what the other people are complaining about."

"I don't see why anyone should complain. You've just said my work has been near perfect. Heaven knows, I try hard enough, especially since we have to get the type of people we do in the supply room."

"Yes, Marjorie, your work has been perfect, but there are some other things that need to be done besides just keeping perfect records."

"Well, I'd like to know what it is! I've spent a lot of time down here on my own making up the right forms for the job. Things are just about at the right place, I think, to almost run themselves. Even with these new people we've got, they can learn pretty quickly with the forms we're using."

"I know, Marjorie, and I've already said a lot of times how proud we are of the job you're doing with these forms, and with the job in general. But I'd like to mention that we have gotten a lot of complaints from the various groups, and some of the complaints have gotten upstairs."

"Upstairs! You mean that someone has gone upstairs to complain about my group? Just let me know what the complaints are about and I'll take care of whichever employee it was."

"Actually, Marjorie, it was, uh, or rather, the complaints were not exactly against your people . . . they, er, were actually, uh, against you."

"Against me! Well, I never heard of such a thing! Who would complain against me? Somebody is just jealous."

"No, the complaints were justified, from what I gather."

"Why me?"

"People are complaining that you give their secretaries such a hard time that they won't come to the storeroom when they need supplies. They say you almost scream at them if they want more than one pencil or pad of paper."

"Well, some of them need to be screamed at. They just come in and ask for two or three boxes when one would do them for a month or more."

"Maybe we haven't made your job duties clear, Marjorie. You aren't to *control* the supplies—that is, see that not too many pencils are used—you are simply to have supplies on hand when someone wants them. Each group must give an account for its own usage."

"I know that, but when they come down in the middle of the month and order more than they should, I have the job of getting more in before my regular ordering time. It messes up my procedures. They could make it a lot easier for me by waiting a few days. I try to tell them that, but they don't seem to care. . . ."

Now what about Marjorie? Is she a good supervisor? When we look more closely at her performance, we see some problems that we didn't see when we looked only at the *results* she was getting. So we can begin to see that results aren't always the best measurement to go by. What is happening here is that Marjorie is so carried away with doing the job a certain way— and doing it well, by the way—that she has forgotten the prime purpose of her job: to be of service to the other groups. We will talk about her supervisor and the appraisal interview in a later chapter. Right now, let's think only about what is a good supervisor. We've added a dimension as we've looked at Marjorie's activities. We've seen that even quality isn't enough, unless the quality is spread over every aspect of the job. We haven't even looked at the morale of the employees working under Marjorie, but we can see from what she's said that she doesn't have a very high regard for them. We see that there is a problem in the other groups, caused directly by Marjorie and her attitude. We see that she's being pretty hard on them because they won't conform to her wishes to keep her own job simple. She has little tolerance for them because they want to get their supplies when they need them, and not when it's convenient for Marjorie to order them. The truth is, we can't say that Marjorie is either good or bad as a supervisor. What we can say is that she is good at some things, bad at some, and average in others. If we looked at her job even more closely, this would become increasingly more obvious. And if we looked at our *own* supervisory skills, we'd see that it would be increasingly true of our own activities. We have to learn to think of supervision as a series of skills— not just one big one.

WHAT IS BAD SUPERVISION?

If we can't say what good supervision is, can we say for sure what bad supervision is? We can say the same thing about each of them. We can say that there are a number of skills, many of which were listed in the beginning of this chapter, and we actually have a *profile* that varies with each skill. We are good at communicating orally, but not so good at writing reports. We are having some trouble doing disciplinary interviews, doing fairly well at delegating work, and finding it easy to run a meeting but very hard to please the boss with our letter writing. In other words, it is just as wrong to think of a bad supervisor as it is to think of a good supervisor, if we can't spell out *what* is good or *what* is bad. Unfortunately, just being a supervisor for awhile doesn't give us an insight into what is good or bad about our own supervision unless we concentrate on it. Also—and this ought to frighten us a little—we can *lose* these skills just as we can learn them. We may have done a very good job of letter writing at one time, but then we may have become careless at it, developed some bad habits, and, without realizing it, ended up very bad at something we were once fairly good at. In a minute we'll talk about getting in and out of ruts, but for right now let's settle the question of good and bad supervision.

Good supervision is a collection of skills that are developed and utilized to an acceptable degree. It does not mean that we have to be perfect. It does not mean that we have to acquire every conceivable skill any supervisor might ever need and be good at it as well. It does mean that we have to learn what skills are required to do the job assigned to us or the job we now hold, and then develop those skills to the degree that we are performing them satisfactorily in the total operation of our job. If that sounds complicated, it really isn't. It simply means that we have to be doing all right at the things we need to do to accomplish our job. We'd say the same thing about a welder or a brickmason. Several skills are required to operate a lathe successfully. We wouldn't just settle for a good finished product if the lathe were torn up because of poor maintenance, or too much waste material resulted from making the product. We look at all aspects of the job, and make our evaluation in terms of its individual parts. The same is true of the supervisor. We say a supervisor is doing a poor job only because certain aspects of the job are being done poorly. It would be a rare person, indeed, who couldn't do *anything* well in the supervisory job.

COMMON CHARACTERISTICS

As has often been observed, there are few characteristics that "good" supervisors have in common. Even when we find common traits, they are exhibited in such different ways that we hardly recognize them as "common." However, we do see some things that they do alike and characteristics that seem to put the successful supervisors ahead of the unsuccessful ones. This being the case, we'd do well to look at our own performances to see if there's something we can improve on. Let's talk about a few of the things that good supervisors do that tend to lead them into successful behaviors.

Good Communicating Skills

Almost everyone agrees that good communication makes better supervision. The reasons are so obvious that we really don't have to give reasons why, especially to those who've supervised in situations where communications were poor. We might look at some of the things successful communicators do that make them good. First of all, they are conscious of the *need* to communicate well. They aren't worried about their egos and are not looking for someone to blame if there's a problem with somebody not understanding something. If they think they've done a poor job of getting a message across, they admit it, back up and try again. They *want* to communicate well. Next, good communicators avoid useless or irrelevant words. Many are convinced that if a few words are good, a lot of words are better, but the good communicator recognizes that—as often as not—words cause misunderstanding as easily as they do understanding. Successful communicators are best known as persons who have something to say. In a meeting, or just in normal conversation, they don't say much but when they do, most people try to get in on what they're saying. They may not be saying any more or saying it any better than anyone else, but because they don't waste words, it's more impressive when they say things than it is when those who talk all the time say them. Next, good communicators practice one of the hardest skills: *they listen.* Books are written on the subject of listening (though sometimes it seems that no one has ever read any of them), so we won't take the time here to expand on all that's required in being a good listener. One thing we do know about good listeners is that they work hard at it. They do all they can to be sure they have the message. They may take notes, they may ask the person speaking to repeat something that's been said, they may ask for an interpretation, or they may repeat what they've heard to be sure it is correct; all of these things help them know if they've gotten the right message. Finally, we see that good communicators always look for feedback on what they've said. They ask people to repeat what was said, they ask for return letters of confirmation to see how their message was understood, and they ask what kind of action their listeners are planning. All of these things help good communicators make sure the message got to the receiver.

Flexibility of Supervising

One advantage the experienced supervisor has over the newer one is the ability to use different styles of dealing with people. The new supervisor is still trying to develop a consistent style. The experienced supervisor has seen enough and has had enough practice with handling different people under different circumstances that flexibility comes easier. Supervising for a long time does not automatically make one good at different styles, but at least the experience is there to build upon. We have to be careful when we say that supervisors need to have flexibility in supervising people, because it may sound like we can supervise anyway we wish. The truth is that we need to be very careful not to become inconsistent in handling people and people problems. Flexibility means altering the way in which someone's situation is dealt with, *with the purpose* of handling it better.

Willingness to Take Responsibility

Responsibility is just another word for "risk." Because of the risk factor, it is somewhat threatening for people to take responsibility. As a result, many people avoid taking any responsibility. They like to have themselves "covered" by someone else so they can at least share the blame for failures, if not avoid it altogether. Good supervisors don't think in terms of failures. Certainly they look at the risks, but they also weigh the value of success against any chance of failure. They go into a situation with one thought in mind: "If it can be done, I can do it." Or they may decide, "If it needs to be done, I'll give it my best shot. If it works, I'll get credit, if not, so be it." There's no substitute for people who are willing to take on a task and go as far as they can with their own abilities. Each of us needs to ask just how willing we are to take risks in order to get the job done. It may well be that at certain times our most important contribution to the organization is that we've been around long enough to understand what has to be done, take on the job regardless of the risk, and see it through. Every boss needs somebody who is there, who is willing to take on even risky and/or unpleasant tasks, and who can be depended on to put the job first and get it done without being watched, rewarded, threatened, or coerced. Successful supervisors are almost always this kind of person.

Deciseveness

"I may not like the solution, but at least I get an answer when I take the boss a problem," or "At least I can get a 'yes' or 'no' when I ask the boss a question." These words of subordinates describe a supervisor who has one of the characteristics that make a supervisor successful. One of the most distressing and frustrating things that can happen, is to have a boss who can't give us an answer. We take in a problem, a letter to be solved, a request for an expenditure, etc.—and then start the waiting game. All the world seems to stand still while the boss goes through the motions of "getting us an answer." Many times what's really happening is that the boss is just indecisive; he or she just can't make decisions as quickly as is necessary when directing the activities of others. Remember, if we find it frustrating and distressing when it happens to us, it's no different when we make it happen to those who work for us!

Ability to Create Empathy

As contradictory as it may seem, successful supervisors have a way of causing others to feel empathy toward them! We have long recognized that good supervisors have empathy for others. They understand that people have problems and try to understand why and how people feel the way they do, but there are those who are able to get others to *understand them*. They are able to communicate some of their own frustrations and problems, and as a result their people tend to be more tolerant of an occasional lack of tact, some harsh words, or even some absence of praise.

Insight Into Others' Behavior

The discussion of empathy brings up a closely related characteristic—insight. There are a few rare and valuable people who can understand the real meaning behind the superficial actions and facades of people. This is different from empathy, because this same insight allows them to look at problems and see causes that others may miss. It also allows them to see solutions that others may not find so obvious. Sometimes it is called wisdom, and perhaps that's a good name for it. Successful supervisors use this trait, or skill, or characteristic to get to the heart of matters, hence they are able to attain workable solutions and better results more quickly than others. There's pretty good evidence that this can be achieved through concentration and practice. The place to start is by asking the question, "Just exactly what is behind all of this?" Or, "Before I go further, what could cause this person to act this way?" It could be that just stopping long enough to ask the questions gives us time to do some reflective thinking, hence giving us more insight than we would have had if we jumped in without looking for a solution.

Others have listed some additional characteristics of successful supervisors, such as high work standards, enthusiasm, commitment to working with people successfully, ambition, etc., but these will give us something to shoot for and to measure ourselves against. We have to understand that the presence of these characteristics doesn't guarantee success, but it certainly increases our chances. On the other hand, the absence of them doesn't automatically doom us to failure, but it does somewhat reduce our chances for success. *We also know that these are absolutes in the sense that we either have them or don't.* We all have them to some degree or another, and we all have different degrees of each characteristic. The goal is to always know what we have, what we need, and what we can work to achieve.

HOW GOOD AM I?

We tend to think of those who have been in the supervisory role for several years as being very sophisticated and possessing a ready grasp of self-evaluation and appraisal. Those of us who have been in this role for awhile know that this isn't the case at all. We know that the hardest thing to do is evaluate ourselves. When we ask ourselves, "How good am I?" we find that the answer doesn't come very easily. How do we tell if we're good or bad? How do we tell if we are getting better or losing the skills we once had? These are important considerations, and we need to know the answers. Let's see if we can find some.

First, we can't begin to tell how well we're doing unless we know what it is we're supposed to be doing. What are the job requirements? As we saw in the case of the staff supervisor, Marjorie had actually lost sight of part of her job. We need to make sure that hasn't happened to us. We need to make sure that we know not only *what* is expected of us but also *how well* we're supposed to perform in that particular task. We need to find out what the standards are for any job we're doing. For example, what about letter writing? Am I supposed to write many letters? Is there a standard for writing these letters? Does the boss think the letters should be written in a particular way? Are my sentences too long to conform with the organization's standards? Am I failing to make the purpose of my letters clear in the first paragraph? Is that what the organization wants in its letters? The process is sometimes complicated, but it's impossible

PECTORALIS
MYTHETUMNIS
ORATHICAN
(EXTINCT)

PERFECT
SUPERVISOR
(RARE BIRD)

for the supervisor to do much about self-evaluation without answering these kinds of questions.

Next, we should look forward to appraisal time. We should want to get the boss's feelings and evaluations. We should even seek information in between the formal appraisal times. It doesn't really matter how well we think we're doing if the organization thinks differently. Hindsight is usually much better than foresight, so let's look behind us at the decisions we made, the interviews we held, the reports we wrote, the messages we gave, and the efforts at motivation we made. Let's look at these things and see whether we did the job as well as the organization wanted us to. When we go into an appraisal session, let's get a list of things the boss is going to be appraising and do our own self-appraisal beforehand. When the session is over, let's check our appraisal of ourselves against that of the boss. And above all, let's not get defensive about any differences. The minute we begin to say, "Well, that's not right," then we're in trouble. We have lost even our twenty-twenty hindsight. As we get older in the supervisory job, several things start to happen. One is that we tend to get defensive. Another is that we get into a rut in both our actions and our thinking.

AM I IN A RUT?

How do I tell if I'm in a rut? Is it a natural disease of experience? Not at all, of course. Many people go all the way to the top of an organization and never get into a rut. Others have that proverbial one year of experience twenty times over, saying they've had twenty years of experience when actually they got into a rut very early and never got out of it. There are some telltale signs, however, and we need to know them. For example, when people just don't seem to be like they used to, then we're in a rut. People change, and if we can't live with that change we're in a rut; like Marjorie, we want everyone to get into step with us. We fail to remember that there were those around who thought *we* were different, and that we used to complain that they didn't let us use our ideas. (We probably said they were in a rut!)

Another indication that we're in a rut is when the organization seems to be making a lot more dumb mistakes. If we find ourselves saying more and more, "I don't see why . . .," then we may be in a rut. If we find that we are reacting to situations without giving them much thought, whether they be appraisals or monthly reports, we are probably in a rut, and may not be doing our job very well. If we find ourselves thinking, "I ought to do more training, but I just can't seem to get around to it anymore," we're in a rut all right, and a serious one at that. If we find it harder and harder to relate to the newer supervisors and their newfangled approaches to supervision, we're in another serious rut. If we find ourselves saying, "I used to worry about the folks taking too long at break, but I've learned to live with it. I just ignore it now," we're in a rut that's bound to hurt us and the organization—and probably already is. There are other signs, but these will give the basic idea. These are serious things, and they can't be ignored. If we expect to perform satisfactorily, we can't do it from inside a rut!

HOW DO I GET OUT OF A RUT?

We accomplish a lot when we find out we're in a rut, and getting out is usually easier than finding out we're in one. In fact, just the very fact that we find that we're in a rut is all it takes to get out of some of them. For example, just realizing that we are overlooking the necessary discipline about breaks, tardiness, or other laxities is enough to get us back on the right track. We used to handle these things in good fashion—how did we do it? The realization gets us back into gear again. This will work for many of the ruts we get into, but not all of them, of course. For the most part, we have to work at getting out. We have to take a long look at ourselves, decide we don't like what we see, and make the diligent effort to get out. This takes effort. Many experienced supervisors have a process that works well for them. They get out a pencil and paper and write down their profile of skills. They then decide whether they're any better or worse in any of these areas than formerly. They decide whether they see themselves as being better at getting along with their fellow supervisors, and whether they are more or less confident in the organization's ability to conduct the operations day in and day out. If they find that there are problem areas in their profile, they concentrate on these areas for several days or weeks. They *consciously* work on getting out of the ruts. They treat their own deficiencies just like they would those of an employee under them. They work on the problem with *specific recognition* of that problem. This is the only way to overcome any deficiency, in supervisor or subordinate.

CONCLUSION

If we haven't learned anything else from supervising for a long period of time, we all know that there's more to the job than just learning a few interpersonal skills. People are complex, supervising people is even more complex, and supervising well is the most complex of all. Experience both helps and hurts us. The experiences we have give us opportunities to learn and to improve, but seeing the same situations repeat themselves over and over again may cause us to relax, get into a rut, and end up doing the same things in the same way without growing.

Our problem may be deciding just how good (or how bad) we are. Since it's difficult to determine just what a good supervisor is, it's hard to find a standard by which to measure ourselves. There are some things that successful supervisors do alike, and to these we direct our attention. If we look at those who are good communicators, and consistently get the job done through others while getting them to enjoy and be committed to their work, then we have a model with which to match ourselves. If these same supervisors have found a way to increase their insight into people and problems, and have it pay off for them, then we have a goal to shoot for.

Mostly, we must see that good supervision is not just getting the job done whatever it takes. There's a big difference between successful supervision and meeting production quotas. The first is lasting and good for the organization; the second may or may not be good for the organization, and may or may not be good for the people under us.

DISCUSSION ACTIVITIES

1. In getting the job done through others, the supervisor needs many different skills. List and define as many of these skills as possible.

2. Separate the skills listed in #1 above into the following categories:
   a. Those that new supervisors often bring with them versus those that nearly always have to be learned
   b. Those that can be easily taught in a classroom versus those that take considerable job experience to learn
   c. Those that must be learned almost immediately versus those that can be developed over the years

3. Discuss (debate) this statement: "In the final analysis, a supervisor is either a good one or a bad one."

4. List ways of telling when a supervisor is getting into a rut.

chapter 2
THE PLACE
OF THE
EXPERIENCED
SUPERVISOR

When a supervisor has been around for awhile, things are different from when the promotion was first made. Different people gradually develop different attitudes and viewpoints. Management sees the person differently. That new supervisor who has just joined the ranks sees the experienced supervisor differently than management does. And the experienced supervisor may see the role differently than when the promotion was made months or years ago. It is important to know these different viewpoints in order to relate better to the various people who must be dealt with rationally day after day.

MANAGEMENT'S VIEWPOINT

When higher management decides to promote a person to the role of supervisor, it is a calculated decision. Managers realize that the decision is only a guess, even though they have given it a lot of thought. They recognize the chance of failure; they know that even though people may have the potential, they may not use the potential. Or there might not be a match between the job and the person, or between the workers and the supervisor. So they naturally watch their decision very carefully. They watch in the hope that it was the right decision, and they watch in order to *prove* it was the right decision. What this means is that those making the decision *want* it to work out. They want the person to succeed in the new job. If we have been promoted, we should find comfort in the fact that we have a few very strong supporters. We shouldn't think we pose a threat to them—we pose more of a threat if we fail than if we succeed. If we don't realize this, we may even get the feeling that there are those who don't care whether we make it, or who even hope we don't make it.

But what about after we've been on the job for awhile? What is the attitude of those above us? Do they still want to see us succeed? What do they expect of us now that we've been on the job for awhile? It would be fair to say that there are many times when they don't think of us at all! This may surprise us somewhat, but there is a thing called "taking us for granted" that takes place when we've been on the job for awhile. When top managers have filled a vacancy, and they see that things are going all right, they just put it out of their minds. They have other problems and other decisions to make. Other areas of the business demand their attention. We find that hard to understand, perhaps, because we think about our job all the time. We wonder how well we're doing; we wonder sometimes if they made the right decision; and we wonder if we're being watched. This is a common failing in most of us. It may not be good for our ego to think that management isn't thinking and talking about us all the time, but it will help us understand the job environment if we can face that fact.

But managers do have a viewpoint about us and the job we're supposed to do. They think about us as able to do the job and notice us only when we fail, except when it is time for appraisal or for another promotion. There's nothing wrong with that viewpoint; it's the way to run a business. *We* make good decisions and then go on to other problems, and the same is true when we've been promoted; management decides to put us in the job, and then tackles another problem. As managers think about us and the job, they often think about us as a part of a smoothly running (hopefully) machine. We have to do our job, and others theirs, to make this whole thing work. Managers *expect* us to do our job, and they've got a right to expect us to do it well. They see us as capable. They see us as experienced and able to handle a problem easily, efficiently, and well. They're only surprised when we mess up. They have none of the anxieties that we have. They have none of our forebodings—*unless we start to mess up the job or the decisions or the morale or the money or the production or the material.*

There are those who say we have to be careful not to rock the boat. They say that management wants things to go smoothly, with no waves. Actually, they're right! Those who say it usually mean it in a derogatory manner, suggesting that management doesn't allow for innovation or change. That happens too, but many times there are disgruntled souls who get burned for rocking the boat a different way. They get in trouble because they didn't do the job they were promoted to. They let things get out of hand, and management had to step in and get things straightened out. There is a story about a mother who expressed concern to the dean of a very large university because her son was not getting personal attention. The dean replied that the only way her son could get personal attention in an organization as big as the university was to bend his computer card. The same is often true in the business world. When one makes it to the supervisory level, the personal attention becomes less and less as the job is handled better and better—*for which we should be grateful!* There are processes through which we get recognized for the good work we do. If there is a job standard for us, and an appraisal system for matching our performance with that standard, we will get the attention we deserve.

Does this mean we just have to keep our noses clean and do nothing? Certainly not. This would show up too, and not many people are rewarded for doing nothing. Maybe we don't get run off, but we won't get ahead, either. Management looks to us for leadership. It expects us to respond to situations with maturity and experience. It expects us to guide and help the newer supervisors and employees. We are the ones who must do much of the training. We also set the standards of performance for the new supervisors, standards as to the kind of treatment the employees will get and, to a certain extent, the *style* of management the organization will have years from now.

THE NEW SUPERVISOR'S VIEWPOINT

New supervisors come into their jobs with apprehension. They feel unsure about their chances of success just as we did when we came into the job. This doesn't mean they are cringing or afraid of their shadow. Nor does it mean they are completely devoid of confidence. It just means that they feel a natural concern about how well they will be able to handle the work assignment. This is especially true if this is their first supervisory assignment. No matter how much supervisory training they may have had, nothing has prepared them completely for what they are about to face. Only experience will give them the final confidence they need—confidence we've gotten from the experiences we've had. It is often up to us to give them the help and guidance that will take them in the right direction. Let's look at the following exchange and see how easy it is for us to influence the newer employees.

Tom is an experienced supervisor—he has been on the job as supervisor of this group for over five years. Sue is new—this is her first supervisory job. Sue comes well prepared for the job; she had experience working in a similar operation at another location while she was going to school, and did very well at it. She decided to move to this town and was interviewed as a new college hire. Considering her previous experience, it was natural to make Sue a supervisor in this group, even though she had not been a supervisor in her previous job. Before coming into the job as supervisor she attended several weeks of management training given to new employees by the organization's training staff. It was the kind of training all the new supervisors get now. Sue has been on the job for about a week, and is talking to Tom at break.

"Actually, Tom, I find it hard to make decisions as quickly as I should. Just today I had one of the fellows come up to me and ask for some time off without taking any leave time or without losing any pay. He said he'd make it up on Saturday—that he'd been doing that before."

"I hope you didn't let him have the time off! He'll worry you to death from now on if you did."

"Well, that's what I mean. I told him I'd have to think about it. What should I have told him?"

"Just do what I do—say no first, then you won't have to think about it."

"He didn't want very much time off—just a couple of hours. He could make that up in a couple of lunch hours.

He sure does a good job for me, Tom. I hate to turn him down."

"Sue, let me give you some good advice. It's something I learned the hard way, and I wish somebody had told me this. If you ever get to thinking about these people as being good guys or bad guys, you're in trouble. You ought to be glad the organization has a policy on something like that. Just tell them you're sorry but no."

"But how can I keep morale up if I act like that?"

"You're not going to keep morale up by letting them do whatever they want. They may not like you but they'll respect you. Be firm. Don't worry if they don't like the decisions you make. They aren't paid to like the decisions. Don't forget, you're a supervisor. They aren't. Don't let them forget that . . . and don't *you* forget it!"

"You know, Tom, I think you've hit on it right there. I keep forgetting I'm not one of the gang. I keep remembering how it was when I was working in the same kind of operation, wondering what the boss had in mind all the time. I think you've really helped me. I'll be glad when I get a little more experience so I can think like you do all the time!"

"Well, I hope you don't get the idea I'm suggesting that you be hard on them—that's not what I'm saying. Just be firm. Pretty soon they'll quit trying to *test* you."

Now let's see what's happened here. We won't try to go into all the aspects of what should have been done; that's not our problem. What we do want to see, though, is how much influence Tom has over Sue. To begin with, Tom has found a system that works for him. He probably hasn't always acted the way he does now, because, like Sue, he was new at one time. Now he speaks with confidence. Now he feels that his system will work every time. He's relatively inflexible now, especially as he talks to the new supervisor. While we seriously doubt that Sue will take on this same confident tone and act just like Tom from now on, we can't help but believe she'll *try* to act like him. Tom's confident tone, his certainty that he has the solution, his experience—all go together to make a good picture for Sue. Even if she had some doubts (and she did express a few in the beginning), they were gone by the end of the discussion. A few more doubts may arise after she gets back and confronts the fellow who asked for time off, but the problem is that she will think it's her own weakness and inexperience that are at fault; she isn't likely to blame Tom's procedure. So now we have a supervisor—a new supervisor—being influenced by an older, more experienced one. If she can make things work for her— that is, if what Tom has suggested even comes close to getting her off the hook next time—she'll be fixed for a long time to come. But what about all those management schools she went to? Didn't they help any? Surely they talked about problems just like these. But maybe the training was too theoretical, or didn't bother with those fringe areas like a couple of hours off without losing pay because it's possible to make up a couple of hours at lunchtime.

Management styles, whether bad or good, have a way of perpetuating themselves through the experienced supervisors. This happens for two reasons. First, managers tend to surround themselves with people who think the same way they do. Autocratic managers like to have autocratic action around them, and encourage and reinforce that kind of behavior; participative managers like to see people under them who allow for participation in the decision-making process. Secondly, there is peer pressure. It's not so much that the pressure is obvious and that new people are afraid to act any other way; it's just that older supervisors seem to have everything worked out, so it's natural for the newer ones to fall in line. When an older supervisor is as positive as Tom, it's hard to imagine that the plan isn't a good one. Since Tom has a good record (or so it would seem to a new supervisor), there's no reason to believe that the action he suggests isn't good sense, and further, that it's anything other than the organization's policy as well. So the new supervisor stands to be greatly influenced by the older ones, *whether the older ones want it or not.*

THINGS THAT HELP

It is not necessarily bad that the new supervisor is influenced by the older ones. We want good supervisors, and if a good one can influence another to act the same way, then so much the better.

"Actually, I never have trouble with insubordination."

But how can we prevent the bad influence as well? It won't help much to tell older supervisors, "Just influence with your good habits, not your bad." Later in this book we'll talk about self-evaluation, but let's pause here and point out the importance of *knowing ourselves.* If there is ever a time to be introspective, it's when we're considering the effect we have on new supervisors. Much of the confidence we exhibit may in fact be a cover-up for our uncertainty. In other words, we may just be putting on a show to protect our ego. Unfortunately, the new supervisor may not be wise enough to figure that out, and may believe we really do have all the answers—as did Sue. While we may sound as though we have everything all worked out, we may not actually be doing all these things as well as *we* think we should, much less as well as they *should* be done. The confidence we show, therefore, may be very misleading to the new supervisor.

A much better way for us to use our experience is to look closely at our performance and admit to ourselves that we aren't doing as well as we should in some areas. Then we will use our influence much more wisely in future discussions with new supervisors. It's not a weakness to admit our shortcomings. By the same token, we can just as easily pass on with great confidence things that work well under different conditions, and that are acceptable to the organization's stated personnel policy. Maybe that was what Tom was doing. If we just recognize that what works for us may not work for everyone, we will be way ahead of the game. If Tom could have just said something like, "Well, I'll tell you something you might try that's worked well for me," then Sue would have at least realized that she was going to have to try out the system for herself. She would also have recognized that not everything that works well for one person works for the next. As experienced supervisors, we simply need to learn to give advice very thoughtfully, realizing that new supervisors can get pretty desperate when situations arise for which they can find no ready answer.

Another valuable attribute for experienced supervisors is the ability to help solve problems without foisting one's own style off on the new supervisors. Let's replay the last scene with a different approach—same setting, same characters, same problem.

"Actually, Tom, I find it hard to make decisions as quickly as I should. Just today I had one of the fellows come up to me and ask for some time off without taking any leave time or without losing any pay. He said he'd make it up on Saturday—that he'd been doing that before."

"Did he say what he wanted the time off for?"

"No, but I'm sure from what he said that it was just some personal business."

"*Has* he been doing it before?"

"I don't know, Tom. I don't even see how I could find out. It wouldn't show up on any of the records, would it?"

"No, I guess not, but you might have asked him if he could give you a specific time when he had done it before, and what the supervisor had said at that time."

"What good would that have done? I couldn't check it out, or at least I wouldn't call Jerry, his former supervisor, and ask about something like that!"

"I know, Sue, but there's no reason to believe that he wouldn't tell you the truth. I've found it works best if I always assume that rather than the other way around. Even if they're trying to test you, they aren't interested in out-and-out lying to you just to get off from work."

"What should I have done? I sure couldn't think of anything right off."

"That's all right, I think, this early in your career as a supervisor. Just don't let indecision get to be a habit with you. I'll tell you what I do. I start off by saying no, and figure that I can change my mind later if I decide the request wasn't so unreasonable after all. You might try this. Of course, my personality is probably different from yours, so what works for me might not work for you. I do know that the organization has some pretty stiff rules about people taking time off without any records being kept. I think they're still a little touchy over that time a person was in a wreck on our time, when he was actually running an errand for a moonlighting job."

Remember, we aren't trying to say what's right or wrong in this case. In fact, we might need to look at Tom's advice in more detail later on, since his is a rather strange solution. But what we're interested in right now is the difference between this approach and the first one. What was different? The main thing is that the advice came with much less assurance that it was the only way to handle the problem. If Sue decides to follow the advice, she'll be doing so with the understanding that though it works for Tom, there is no guarantee it will work for her. She's also been advised that she'd better experiment, rather than accept this advice as infallible. One of the best things Tom did was to do a little probing. He asked questions for which Sue needed answers. Tom has learned that you can gain a little time, and a lot more information, by asking some questions. Hopefully, the next time Sue is faced with a decision, she'll ask some questions, too. Not challenging ones. Not questions designed to nail the employee to the wall. Just questions that will give more insight into the problem. As the employee gives us more information, we have a chance to think and put things into proper perspective. That's an important aspect of problem solving, and Sue would be fortunate if she learned this valuable lesson from an experienced supervisor.

We should also point out the influence that the experienced supervisor had on Sue—or hopefully will have—with the advice about assuming that employees are telling the truth unless and until proven otherwise. Again, we have to be careful here not to get into the problem too much, since our subject is the influence an experienced supervisor can have on a new one, but what better example could we find than this? It's a casual thing. Tom didn't make a big deal out of it—he simply said, "I've found it works best." In other words, he's saying that it may not work for Sue, but it works for him. He's also saying that he had to find out what works best for him, and that Sue will have to do the same.

So far we've been talking about the experienced supervisor's influence on new supervisors. We should also point out that one of the things that helps the organization use the talents of the older, experienced supervisors is for the supervisors to express to the newcomers, early in the game, an interest in following the organization's policies. This doesn't have to be a flag-waving ceremony. It's not a matter of showing blind faith in everything the organization does. It is a matter of taking a mature stand on those things the organization has decided to do, and seeing that energies are best utilized toward those goals. An organization has only a certain amount of energy to expend, and any that is used up in poor morale, fighting the policies, and efforts at creating ill will against the organization will surely keep the end goals from being achieved as quickly as they could otherwise. Experienced supervisors can be a big asset in keeping things smoothed over, if for no other reason than that the newer persons respect the ideas of the older, more seasoned people—providing they are used well, as we'll see later in this chapter.

THINGS THAT HURT

Now let us look at some problems that are bound to arise with supervisors who have been around a long time. One common fault is that we start to use our experience as a defense against learning new things. We tend to worry about those who are coming in behind us, especially as they have more and more supervisory training. We see them finding new approaches to problems, talking about things with a different management vocabulary. We feel that we may be getting behind them in some ways, so we start saying things like, "Well, that stuff may sound good, but experience is still the best teacher." As we'll see in a minute, this is a deadly sign that we're getting into trouble. It's simply a defense mechanism coming to light and we need to learn to recognize it as quickly as possible.

Another problem that hinders our progress and keeps us from making the best use of our experience is our failure to actually observe our own progress. There are many who do the right things, but don't profit from them. They really never stop to analyze *what* they did that worked and *why* it worked. One reason we find ourselves saying things like, "I guess you just have it or you don't when it comes to supervision," is that we don't realize that we've set up a pattern (or habit) of supervision without really knowing it. We're more likely to repeat those things that cause us the least trouble and avoid those things that cause us the most trouble. We can set up these habits unconsciously, and the trouble is that we can just as easily set up bad habits as good ones. "But wait a minute," someone says. "I thought you said that we find out what *works,* and then repeat these things." No, that's not what we said. We said that we find out what causes us the *least trouble,* and repeat those things. And what causes us the least trouble often isn't the best thing by a long shot. For example, if we have trouble making a decision, we may find that stalling people off—telling them we'll have to think about it for awhile—may cause people just to quit asking us to make decisions. They either don't do anything, or they do what they want to do, or they just muddle through in some way. Whatever they do, they'll find a way to avoid asking us for a decision if they possibly can. This makes it easier for us, but certainly doesn't mean that this is the best way to handle our decision-making chores.

Not all the problems that surround us as the experienced people in the group are of our own making. We've already pointed out that people see us differently when we have been around for a longer period of time. Unfortunately, there are those who, instead of seeing our experience as helpful, are suspicious of us because we've stuck around and haven't moved on to some other job. No matter what the reason for our still being on the same job, there are those who will think the worst of us. Whatever their reasons, we have to be careful not to fall into the trap of making their suspicions come true. We don't want to appear cranky, hard to get along with, or full of idiosyncrasies. We don't want to become demanding of our "earned rights." If people have to treat us "just right" or we'll flair up at them, then we've fallen into that trap—perhaps without even knowing it. It is very easy to begin to act the way people expect us to. If people expect us to be hard to get along with, we'll find ourselves acting that way unless we make a special effort to avoid it. The most profitable thing for us to do is overcome this "expectation of the worst" by giving the opposite reactions whenever possible. We can be almost overly cooperative. We can be helpful, open, and especially friendly to the newer people. If we work at it, this won't be an act; it will be a part of us. This doesn't mean we become spineless jellyfish; it means we are considerate of others' needs and rights. It means we do not demand things *just because we've been around awhile.*

USING EXPERIENCE INSTEAD OF TENURE

Let's listen to a situation that is repeated often in many organizations. Alan Borden has been around for a number of years. He's a supervisor in an office and is in charge of about ten people. He was hired several years ago through the college hiring program, but at a time when there wasn't much movement upward due to slow growth. Most people who were hired during this period have remained at the same level, as has Alan. In recent years, though, some upward movement has begun. Several people of the same vintage as Alan have been promoted, as well as some who were hired since him. Alan's present boss was hired about the same time as Alan, was promoted a year ago to head up another office, and has just recently—in the last three months—been moved in to head up this office. As he began to look at the way things were organized, the boss realized that Alan's experience was invaluable, and that much of the work flow was dependent on Alan. The problem was that Alan's desk was in the back of the room, out of the normal flow. Alan supervised from back there, and from his standpoint this arrangement seemed to serve very well. He could see the people, was available if they had questions, and liked the quiet atmosphere in that location. It was generally considered a "prestigious" location, since those with the most seniority moved to that portion of the room. Alan's boss has just called him into the office:

"Come in, Alan. Hope I'm not interrupting anything critical."

"No, no problem at all, Dan. Needed a break anyway. Haven't looked up from the paperwork all morning."

"I notice you spend a lot of time that way. You really turn out the work back there!"

"Well, thanks. There sure seems to be enough to turn out these days. I remember when we did less work in a week than we now do in a couple of days."

"That's true. And people are always talking about the old days when people had to work so hard. I'd pit this office against any of the ones a few years ago."

"Yeah, me too, Dan. Of course, we've got a better crowd of people, I think. We're hiring a lot of pretty sharp young folks. A fellow has to stay on his toes to just keep up these days. I don't mind telling you, though, it's good to hear you say that about these folks."

"Well, it's not just me, Alan. I heard how good they were —how good *you* were—before I even moved here. What I wanted to talk to you about, though, is some changes I have in mind for the work flow."

"Oh? Is there something wrong with what we've been doing? Or is it the way we've been doing it?"

"No. There's nothing wrong with the way you've been doing the work, and there's certainly nothing wrong with *what* you've been doing. I've just been looking at the work flow, drawing up a chart or two, and it seems to me that there must be a better way to move the work around the office. Most of your people are all together toward the back, Mildred's people are around her, and Sam's up toward the front. That's pretty good from a supervisory standpoint, but it plays havoc with the work flow."

"It seems to me things flow pretty well. We don't have any trouble in my group."

"Well, there's not so much trouble within any one group. It's just that when you start putting the groups together, as I have to do, things don't flow as well as they should. What I've been thinking is that you and your group are really the key to moving things out of here. Everyone else has to pass their stuff through you. What I thought was that we could make better use of your whole outfit if we could move you up where Sam is, let Mildred take your location, and Sam take her's."

"Hey, wait a minute! You're not suggesting that we re-shuffle the whole office, are you?"

"It does just about come to that. That's why I wanted to talk to you about it first. I haven't mentioned this to anyone else. I wanted to get your reaction first."

"I can give it to you in a hurry. I don't like it. Maybe that's not the right thing to say, but I've been around long enough to have some rights, and frankly, the place where my desk is—and where my people are—suits me just fine. I think it suits them fine too!"

"Wait a minute, Alan. I don't mean to get you upset. We don't have to make the move. Maybe you've got a better suggestion. I just thought it would give us a chance to utilize your group a little better and move the work around better."

"Well, you've already said we move it pretty well as is, and I can't see doing all that moving just to upset the way we've been doing things. I guess seniority doesn't mean much when you get to be a supervisor."

We'll stop the story there. We've heard enough to get the feel for the way things will go from here on out. What's the problem? It's not enough to say that maybe Dan didn't use a very good approach—already having the plan worked out before calling Alan in. He at least talked to Alan first, before talking to anyone else. We can't even pass it off by saying that Alan had a bad attitude. He did, but why? What was wrong with his attitude? Was he just old and set in his ways? Was he resentful of Dan's coming in over him? We may not know the answers to all these questions, but we can answer some of them. We can at least see where Alan's values were, and how they got in his way at decision-making time. First, let's notice that he had some things going for him. He wasn't wedded to the past. "The good old days" didn't hold much for him, and he wasn't hung up with the idea that the new folks coming on board were all bad, which is a problem with many older supervisors. Next, he was well thought of, even outside of the group. Dan had "heard about him, even before he came here." Also, he was quite willing to give his people credit for the work they were doing. Putting all this together, we have a pretty good prospect for success. The fact that Dan wanted to make better use of Alan and his group suggests that the organization was ready to give Alan a better opportunity to show what he could do. So what went wrong?

The problem stemmed from the fact that Alan let his seniority overshadow his future. He was using his tenure instead of his experience to make decisions. His experience should have told him that Dan's proposal made a lot of sense. It should have also told him that if he didn't like the move, Dan respected him enough to listen to some alternatives. As it was, he pretty well shut the door to further discussion on the matter. If the move is made anyway, Dan will have to live with the embarrassing fact that he had to do it in spite of Alan's objections. If the move isn't made, Dan will most likely hold future unsatisfactory work-flow situations against Alan. Alan has perhaps saved his status symbol—the location of his desk—but he may have sacrificed a part of his future to win the battle. It may have been a costly victory!

CONCLUSION

Being an experienced supervisor puts us in a unique position. We have some privileges that come with "age," and we have some problems that are generated by our having been around "too long." Management looks to us for work, solutions, help, and guidance of newer employees—new supervisors. They expect us to succeed and they may not even recognize our existence until we cause some type of problem. At the same time, they may appear to spend more time training and developing younger or less experienced supervisors at our expense. They may even appear to be grooming someone for the higher job above us, even asking us to do much of the grooming. That's all right. Our job is to make certain that we do our job enthusiastically and well, and always show a loyalty to the organization.

At the same time that we're trying to find our "niche" in the organization, others have already decided where they think we should be. Also, there are new things happening that make it imperative for us to change our place in the organizational structure. Far from being in a stagnant situation, we're actually in one in which we can have a tremendous impact on everything that happens. Even the new supervisors eventually look to us for direction. Of course this has some drawbacks for us because management expects us to "steer them right." This may mean we can't do as much complaining about policies as we'd like or just sit back and live on our past accomplishments. We have to keep our knowledge of what's going on current, even in those areas where we aren't directly involved. It may mean that we don't get the recognition we think we deserve, or even worse, that others may receive the credit for our work or decisions. However, that's our role as experienced supervisors, and the evidence is rather overwhelming that in the long run it'll benefit us.

DISCUSSION ACTIVITIES

1. List the advantages *and* disadvantages of the fact that higher management actually wants very much for the newly promoted or appointed supervisor to succeed in the new job.

2. Discuss (debate) this statement: "Top management will know it a lot quicker when we mess up than when we do our job well."

3. What advantages *and* disadvantages do experienced supervisors have over new supervisors when it comes to decision making *where there is no policy*?

4. What problems arise for the experienced supervisor just as a natural result of *being around for a long time*?

5. Looking at the problems listed in #4 above, list some ways of preventing each from happening.

6. In what ways can the experienced supervisor influence the new supervisor's action and attitude *without even talking about that particular subject or action*?

chapter 3
GETTING RIGHT WITH MANAGEMENT

In this chapter we want to continue to look at some things that may be a problem with experienced supervisors, things that may keep us from getting ahead, from performing our jobs properly, or from simply getting the recognition we deserve for what we're able to contribute. Mostly, we want to concentrate on our relationship with our management. As experienced supervisors, we have been around long enough to understand the importance of knowing and respecting top management's policies and practices. But there are some kinds of thinking that will keep us from being as successful as we deserve to be or are capable of being. Let's see if we can determine what they are.

"I SHOULD HAVE BEEN PRESIDENT" SYNDROME

It would be interesting to see how many people there are in any organization who think they should have been promoted long ago, and to a much higher job. The symptoms sound like this:

"I knew him when he was still unable to find his way to the washroom."

"She used to have to ask me how to fill out the monthly time sheet, and look where she is now."

"Both of them together can't make one good decision; I can run circles around them on almost any phase of the business."

"He must have known somebody—he couldn't have made it on his own."

These kind of statements are heard every day, over and over again, in most organizations. Who are the people doing the talking and who are they talking about?

First, the ones doing the talking are usually the ones who feel they've somehow been passed over. The reasons that they were passed over may or may not have been made clear to them; but for one reason or another, they've put the reasons out of their minds—if they ever knew them. As they look at the organization chart and see people at higher levels than themselves, they begin thinking about these people who've made it, and remember things about them from bygone days. They remember when these people first came on board, or the times when the now-higher-level person asked *them* a question or sought advice. They feel a trace of resentment, a dash of jealousy, a pinch of bitterness, and perhaps a heap of frustration. It is unlikely that their comments are completely factual; those in higher positions aren't simpletons, devoid of intelligence and reason. While those who are frustrated perhaps could do more than they're now doing, and could handle more responsibility (most people can), it is unlikely that they could move into a top-management job and perform without some error or poor judgement. (If they could, then the organization has a very poor system for recognizing and promoting talent!) But it's awfully easy to sit back and imagine that we could handle a much higher job. After all, what's so difficult about those jobs? All they do up there is pass the work down to us. When we begin to think in those terms, we are beginning to get the first blushes of the "I should have been president" syndrome.

Now who are the people in higher management who are being talked about? All of them, of course, but the things that distinguish them are that (1) they got promoted, and (2) they can't just *imagine* how it would be to make decisions, they actually have to *make* them. Being in a decision-making position puts us all in the spotlight; we rarely please everybody and seldom find that people appreciate the difficulty that goes into making good decisions. For this reason, it's easy for people to take potshots at those who get promoted up to higher levels of management. But those who get promoted are unique in ways other than simply that they got promoted. A closer examination usually shows that they handled their jobs well at lower levels. They made good decisions over smaller problems and somebody saw this as good evidence that they could handle bigger problems. They were probably good at planning, organizing, communicating, and all those other skills that make good managers—not perfect and not without weaknesses, but good enough to get the job done and a little more. More than anything, they showed an understanding of management's problems and could identify with these problems. They could relate their own work to these problems and offer solutions to the extent they were asked to do so.

Furthermore, these people were no doubt sympathetic with the organization's problems and with top management's efforts to solve them. This doesn't mean that they were simply yes-men and yes-women, or that they had no disagreement with what top management was doing, or that they thought top management never made any mistakes. Nor does it mean that they gave up their rights to individual opinions and thoughts. They didn't "sell out," as it were—they were *sympathetic* with management's efforts. We touched on this in the last chapter when we talked about understanding management's viewpoint. The one thing we can never afford to do is get into the feeling that it is *us against them* in terms of ourselves and top management. We have enough of that *below* us not to start it above us too.

"MANAGEMENT OUGHT TO KNOW BETTER" SYNDROME

Closely akin to the "I should have been president" syndrome is that feeling that surely management just overlooked us. Management really ought to know better than to promote these *other* people, make decisions like that, or run the organization the way they do. Of course, there are very few of us who would agree with management about everything, and it is rare that even management will claim that it has *always* made the right decisions about people, about promotions, and about who *not* to promote. It would be presumptuous, however, to conclude that just because we didn't make it, and someone else did, management made the wrong decision. We may not like the decision; we may think we are better prepared, better able to handle the next-higher job; we may think we can do our own job with our hands tied behind us. But none of this proves that we really are the one for the job. As we will say many times in this book, top managers—those who make promotion decisions—are privy to much more information about people and things than we are. The decision makers may even have more information about *us* than we do! They have information on us that is organized, categorized, and relatively unbiased. Even though we obviously have more total facts about ourselves, we probably don't have very much *unbiased* information about ourselves. Nor do we have very much organized information—ours is all jumbled together, unrelated to itself in many ways. Futhermore, we see ourselves as we used to be, which isn't related to the present or future except as a cause or reason for some of our actions. And finally, we see ourselves as we wish we were, with all our ambitions, wants, desires—which may explain our motivation but does not reveal our real capabilities. As we will see later on, it's very difficult to see ourselves as we actually are, free of any prejudice. Our managers, however, do not have this problem, since they have usually devised systems to give them reasonably good data about us, free from the biases we develop living with ourselves for all of our lives!

The problem with developing this "managment ought to know better" syndrome is that we spend a lot of time thinking about it, and maybe talking about it, and we *end up getting bitter.* Once that happens, all bets are off, because we are no longer really qualified to take a higher job. Bitterness is something that creeps up on us, making us undesirable to ourselves, those around us, and the organization we work for. While it may be easy to spot bitterness in others, it's quite difficult to spot it in ourselves. What do we mean by "bitterness"? Let's look at some typical phrases that come from bitter supervisors:

1. "It doesn't matter what you do around here; only the fair-haired boys get the promotions."
2. "I don't care how hard you work; if you don't have a fancy degree, you won't make it in this organization."
3. "It's not what you do that gets you ahead; it's who you know."
4. "I've knocked myself out, and that lazy slob hasn't had a

"Oh, I could have been director of the whole thing—but you known how office politics go!"

good workday since she showed up—and she gets the job!"

5. (To new employee) "You'd better recognize early that it pays to be nice to everybody around here, because there's no logical way to tell who you might be working for one of these days."

We recognize these statements as coming from people who are bitter; their bitterness shows right through the conversation. Let's look at them one at a time and see what's really being said, what kind of damage is being done. In case 1, we see the symptoms showing up in the description of who it is that gets ahead. The name-calling of "fair-haired" people gives the supervisor away, although the whole statement reeks with problem thinking. It implies that you are not appreciated for doing your job. Promotions go to those who get "branded" early and the rest of us poor souls might as well forget about any kind of reward. Now even if there is an element of truth to this, the fact that we say these things shows that we have given up, in a sense, and are using this kind of thinking to rationalize our poor performance. (Or we may still be just a step away from turning in a poor performance.) The process of disintegration goes something like this: First, we may think the organization can do no wrong. Then we see some mistakes, but overlook them because we still think the organization is basically good. Next we begin to let the supposed mistakes get through to us, and our work may begin to suffer. Finally, our work does suffer, but we can easily blame the organization for its poor policies, practices, and decisions. We have been overcome by bitterness.

In case 2, we find the same "language" problem. The expression "fancy degree" smacks of bitterness against someone who has gotten ahead who does have a better degree than us or more education. Too much has been said about getting ahead purely on degrees, so we won't add to that here except to point out that "It's sometimes possible to get uneducated up through the Doctor's degree!" What we want to talk about here is the matter of letting ourselves become bitter because someone gets ahead who does have more degrees or a better education than we do. First of all, we rarely know for sure exactly why someone else gets promoted or gets better treatment than we do. If we listen to rumors or start to use our imagination, only the worst can result. As horrible as it sounds, we also have to face the fact that the person may just be better qualified than we are, *even because of education*. When we start making remarks like example 2, casting aspersions on education, we're showing our bitterness. The sins of bitterness are hard to forgive because—as in this case—they quite often are directed against the organization as well as the people in the organization.

This thought is best illustrated in case 3, however. Here we see the bitterness aimed at the basic integrity of the organization. What we're really saying is that the organization actually plays favorites, basing decisions on this favoritism rather than on the qualifications of the individuals. This implies that the organization is dishonest, unfair, and not worthy of our best efforts. If we really believe this, then there is little likelihood that we'll put in many fulltime days for our full-day's pay. When this has happened, we rarely are qualified for the next job. We can only go on being bitter, being overlooked for the next opening, becoming even more bitter, and finding ourselves getting very little satisfaction out of coming to work. As a matter of fact, we'll find that the days can get awfully long when we get to feeling this way.

Before we go on to the next case, we have to defend the action of promoting the people we know, as case 3 suggests. The truth is, we *do* promote those we know over those we don't know. We all realize that when two people are essentially equal in job capabilities and qualifications, we're much more likely to choose someone we know well than someone we aren't as well acquainted with. There's nothing wrong with this, providing the people being considered are actually about equal.

The fact that managers promote those they know suggests that we give some consideration to how people get to be known in an organization. In this instance, we aren't talking about "buttering up" the boss; we're talking about other ways to get recognition. While the most obvious way is to do an outstanding job all the time (nothing has been found to work more consistently than this), there are some other things that work pretty well. For example, we can acquire a reputation for being willing to tackle difficult assignments. While everyone else is ducking the assignment, we can put ourselves in the forefront by not complaining when we have an opportunity to do a job that requires special attention to details or a bit more effort on our part. Another possibility is by using a little *imagination* to solve problems. While tried-and-true methods got that way because they worked, there are times when a little creativity will go a long way toward winning us some recognition. We aren't talking about far-out, wild suggestions, but about solid ideas that should work and that are obviously good solutions when they are given a chance to work. How do we get these kinds of ideas? By not becoming blinded by the everyday activities of the job. By backing off *mentally* every once in awhile, and looking at the whole picture to see just what the problem is and what will solve it. Later we'll be talking about problem solving and decision making, which will give us an opportunity to look at this in more detail, but for now we'll just say that good ideas are welcome in more situations than they show up in.

A final way to become known in the organization is to come on with a positive attitude as often as possible. When an idea is suggested by the boss, by others we work with, or by those who work for us, what is our *first* reaction? Is it a positive one? Do we start thinking of ways the idea will work, or do we start thinking of reasons why it won't work? This is especially important with regard to new organizational policies or procedures. When the boss passes on a suggestion or gives us an assignment to do that's a little different from our normal way of doing things, we should train ourselves to think about the good side of the idea or suggestion rather than the bad side. Many managers pick their promotions from those people who come on with the positive approach—who have the attitude of "Here's what it will take to make this work" rather than "Here's why that won't work." This doesn't mean that we shouldn't test the ideas, or that we should just agree and become a yes-man or yes-woman to anything the boss says. Nor does it mean that we shouldn't rise up and voice our opinions if we think something is wrong with an idea. It does mean that we should give serious consideration to any ideas, and that we shouldn't reject an idea or procedure just because we've always done it a different way.

Now let's look at case 4. Here we're back in the name-calling business again. The bitterness is showing through very strongly, in two ways. There's some self-pity in the statement, "I've knocked myself out," which is really a way of saying, "I've been somewhat of a martyr, and now I'd like to go back and collect what's coming to me." Most of us recognize—when we stop and think about it—that we usually have to stop with *self*-pity, since we're the only ones who can build up much interest in pitying us. When we begin to talk about how hard we've worked, we end up scaring people away from us, since few people get much excitement out of listening to us talk about how much we've sacrificed for the organization. They realize more quickly than we do that we're feeling sorry for ourselves, and they don't want to indulge us in that pastime. The important thing is to realize that such self-pity is the beginning of bitterness, and should put us on guard right away. We can stop bitterness before it consumes us, but it's difficult to go back to being loyal to the organization when bitterness has gotten a good hold on us. It's also difficult to regain the confidence of the people around us when we've expressed ourselves in "bitterness" terms.

But there was more to this case than just self-pity. There was the matter of name-calling again. "That lazy slob" isn't exactly a flattering expression. It doesn't do much to inflate the ego of the person being talked about, and we've got to assume that such statements *will* ultimately get back to the person we're describing. Notice all the accusations in this one sentence: "Lazy," meaning the person lacks energy and self-starting ability; "slob," meaning that the person is somehow undesirable; "hasn't had a good workday," suggesting that the person has accepted money under false pretenses; and, "she gets the job!" implying that the person in no way deserves the promotion. That's a pretty serious set of charges! Underlying all of this is the built-in accusation that management is unjust, unfair, not very observant, and very poor at decision making. Only a very bitter person could put all these charges in one short statement.

Case 5 should get us removed from the job, if it represents our kinds of statements. It's not much different from the other statements, but the fact that it's made to a *new employee* is intolerable. There's no way we could ever back off and excuse such a statement, perhaps even if it were true! Let's get a breakdown of all that's being said to this new employee in this statement. First, remember that the speaker is an *experienced* supervisor. The new employee may or may not be a part of the supervisory force—there are implications either way—and there is every reason to believe that the new employee will get his or her ideas from this experienced supervisor. Here is a person with years of experience, apparent respectability, and a knowledge of the company or organization saying that the company or organization has no reasoning or logic behind its promotional policies. That's pretty damning. Even worse, it's a serious thing to say to a new person just coming on board with a relatively clean slate as far as biases are concerned. Finally, this statement smacks of bitterness of the worse kind: the implication that things just sort of mysteriously happen, without anyone being in on the decision except a very few select people. That's not likely to give the new employee much confidence in the way the organization is run or in the contribution a new employee can make to the total decision-making process of the organization.

So, where are we with this matter of bitterness? We've found that it does us no good—it's not even a very good way to let off steam—and it doesn't make us any more popular with the people around us, whether they be peers, bosses, or subordinates. We become bitter, then begin to justify the people who might have passed us over for promotion. Even if it wasn't so in the beginning, when we get bitter and let it show we end up proving the people right who chose to by-pass us on this occasion.

GIVING MANAGEMENT A FAIR CHANCE

If we've learned anything as experienced supervisors, we should have learned that the people running the organization aren't perfect. Yet is it fair to spend much time on their imperfections? Probably not. What we need to learn to think about is their overall batting average. How well do they do in general? What have they done well lately? What have they excelled in? What surprises have they pulled that really smacked of genius? And even though we may kid about it, we don't have to look too far to see these things, especially *if we want to find them.* Perhaps the most difficult thing for supervisors at any level and at any given time to understand is the fact that higher management always has better information than we do, no matter how much *more* we have. We have to understand that just knowing a lot about how people are thinking at our level, or what the gripes are, or what the job difficulties are, or what it is that customers complain about the most, still doesn't give us all the information we need to make sound judgments. Top managers have access to things that we usually don't. They know more about the money policies; they know more about the organization's goals (even in a "participative" environment); they know more about the business world around us; they know more about the direction of similar organizations—the ones we must follow or the ones we must get ahead of; and they know more about how to follow or how to get ahead. Furthermore, they have more of the total picture of this organization than we do. We're just in one department or group. We're seeing things through the limitations of our work group while they see the results of all the work groups put together. While it may end up being confusing, it also ends up giving them a better look at the organization than we get from our vantage point.

What can we do as experienced supervisors to make higher management's job easier? We can give managers a chance to prove their worth, taking into consideration the things we've just said about their access to more valuable information. We can be quicker to approve than to disapprove. We can try to reach back into our experience bank and see what knowledge we've got that would explain the reasons why things are being done the way they are. We also can make an honest effort to get ourselves out of the "judgement seat" of deciding what is right and what is wrong. We can do this by exercising a little patience and accepting the fact that there is always the chance— remote though it may be—that *we* could be wrong! It takes a great deal of patience on our part just to be a part of the organization, especially when we've been around for a long time. We've seen policies come and go. We've seen contradictions, overlaps, gaps, confusion, and internal fighting and politics;

we've seen general ineptness being rewarded and competence being ignored. But in the face of all this, we still see good things. Above all, we're still here. We have to be careful not to say that only the bad guys stay around, since we're still here. We have to avoid saying that anybody can be a supervisor, with or without skill, since we're a supervisor ourselves. This all is to say, "Give management a fair chance." We'll talk about this all along as we have occasion, but one thing we can establish as a general rule right here is that if we are given a job to do and our reaction is "This will never work," then it probably won't. On the other hand, if our reaction is "Let's get on with it," then we'll probably make it work. If we believe that management is made up of people just like us—with both good and bad traits—and we give them all the support we can, we not only will help them out, we're bound to help ourselves as well.

SUPERVISING, NOT DOING

One thing we can do to make management's jobs easier is to spend more time tending to people and less time doing technical things. Newly promoted supervisors, especially those from within the ranks, can be expected to concern themselves with the technical aspects of the job. They're usually more comfortable with *things* than with people, because most of the time they haven't had the experience of doing things *through* people.

We've been away from the technical, day-to-day, hands-on job. We feel more comfortable about getting others to do the actual work, and are accustomed to the frustration of trying to get people to do things that we could probably do better and more quickly ourselves. We've even learned to live with the risk of delegating tasks to less capable people, even when we are likely to be blamed if the job doesn't go well. Due to this experience, we can serve management well by helping the newer supervisors learn how to work through others. Of course, the best way to do this is by setting an example. We are paid to be supervisors, not to do the job. We are earning our keep if we do what supervisors are supposed to do.

The problem we often have with all of this, is that every once in a while we also need the satisfaction of *doing*. With the newer attitudes of the present work force, with the restrictions and policies on employment, with the regulations on what we can and can't do for and with employees, and with the lack of tangible evidence of accomplishment when we delegate, we finally get to the point where we'd like to go out and drive a nail, make a box, or type a letter just for the satisfaction of knowing that we have done something right. That's not an uncommon feeling, even among executives, and occasionally it's all right to succumb to such yearnings. The restrictions are that we can't violate work rules or policies, or get in the habit of doing it too often. What we can do for management is to help new supervisors over the hump into the world of less tangible results. One thing we can be sure of: the bosses of the new supervisors are going to be tearing their hair out trying to get these new people to do more delegating, just as they did when we first became supervisors. Any help from us will be greatly appreciated!

LETTING INFORMATION FLOW

Another favor we can do for management is insure the efficient flow of information in any areas under our control. Simply stated, our job is to let the people under us know what they should be doing and to inform higher management about what they have accomplished. We send down information on policy, goals, decisions, plans, and budgets; we send up information on the results we've gotten by using the people under us. This upward flow helps management in the controlling aspects of their job and helps them measure their progress toward the goals and long-range plans they've set. Since all of this is an ongoing process, as they review our material, we will receive information back from them regarding how to proceed.

All of this works fine, providing we do our part in sending them the information they need and use the information they send us wisely. We are a vital link in the supervisory chain. If we hold on to too much information, without putting it to work wisely, then our people will be unable to do their jobs properly. They will flounder, doing things incorrectly without knowing it until it's too late; they will become disenchanted with our system because they'll feel we're holding out vital information from them; and they will become unmotivated, saying, "Why bother? Let them do it themselves since they don't trust us." We will have unhappy, uninformed employees doing a poor job—all because we failed to supply them with the information necessary to do their jobs.

It works the other way, too. If we fail to keep higher management informed, they'll make many of the same mistakes as the people below us. They'll make plans for the future based on partial information, they'll set unrealistic goals because they won't know some of the things that failed to work before, and they'll "under-budget" or "over-budget" because they won't know what really happened to the money they allocated in the previous budget period. (Naturally, we can "hide" the bad news for just so long, especially as far as money is concerned, but harm can be done if we hide it for even a short time.) It's a natural thing for us to try to keep bad news from our bosses, and some of them make it easy for us. Just as the emperor once killed those who brought bad news, bosses today make the bearer suffer, even if it's not his or her fault. But even in the face of possible repercusions, we still have an obligation to make every effort to get necessary information to the right people. In fact, if we can only get one kind of news to the boss, we should opt for the bad news. Good news will be welcome anytime, but bad news usually requires some immediate action.

CONCLUSION

What is the task of the experienced supervisor in any organization? It's one of getting our thinking right and ending up on management's team. It's one of deciding that we can make things work out all right, even if we've been overlooked for someone we don't think is as capable as we are. The task is to see that we get our viewpoints lined up parallel with management's. There's nothing to be gained by sitting in the back of the boat and paddling in the opposite direction just because we don't like the way the others are paddling—or don't like the paddlers! The biggest danger we face if we don't take on these attitudes is to become bitter. Once this happens, we may be sentenced to a long and unpleasant life of wishing and dreaming for a life that may never be, but could have been if we hadn't messed up our own chances by becoming bitter in the first place.

DISCUSSION ACTIVITIES

1. List symptoms of confused thinking processes with regard to the organization, as far as the experienced supervisor is concerned.

2. Experienced supervisors frequently become "bitter old supervisors" in the eyes of management. List behaviors that might cause higher management to take this view of a supervisor.

3. Still thinking of the bitter supervisor mentioned above, give reasons why these supervisors get that way.

4. Discuss (debate) this statement: "It doesn't matter that the organization *made* these supervisors bitter . . . the supervisors will still have to be appraised on the basis of their own performance."

5. Discuss the merits of a supervisor who looks at a proposal on the basis of why it can't be done versus one who approaches the problem from the basis of what it will take to get the job done. What are the hazards of each approach?

chapter 4

MAINTAINING A MANAGEMENT STYLE

We hear a lot about management "style," but often we really don't know what we mean by the term. We are aware that other people have a style of management, but often don't think of ourselves as having one. We tend to do what comes naturally, thinking that after all, "managing is really just a matter of common sense." The conclusion is that we must have plenty of common sense, because we usually think of ourselves as being pretty good managers. We could always be better, of course, but just look at all those others out there who aren't as good as we are! (We may not verbalize it quite like that, but perhaps more than we would like to think, we do feel that way.) The best way to examine our own management style is to look at what style is, what it takes to develop a style, and what it takes to change one after we get it.

WHAT IS "STYLE"?

When we think of a management style, we're actually talking about the everyday us, the person we are when we aren't thinking about style. Our style is what we do on a normal day under normal conditions with normal problems. That's us, and that's our style. But style is more than just the normal things we do. If we check, we'll see that we are "normal" at other times, too. For example, when we're under stress, there are probably things we invariably do: get mad, become frustrated, remain calm, get excited, start blaming others, become irritated, and so on. We have a reaction that is typical of us, and that's our style of managing under stress.

If we want to know our style, we have to know how we react under stress—but not *only* under stress. How do we react to whatever stimulus comes along? Do we act differently under different stimuli? Do we treat some people differently than others? For example, do we treat the person who tries hard better than the person who does just enough? Do we show disgust when a person who is capable of doing much more does only a halfway job? Do we ignore people coming in late from break or leaving early to go home? That's our style, if we do it consistently. On the other hand, we may find that we're not sure just what to do, so sometimes we do one thing and sometimes another. This may suggest that we haven't developed a firm style yet, or worse, that we may have developed a wishy-washy style. We may have become jellyfish managers, and even though we think we will get better someday (when we have more experience), the chances are slim that we'll get better all by ourselves by just being around as supervisor. Our changes will come gradually and *without purpose* unless we give them some assistance and direction. What we're saying is that whatever the *real us* is, that's our style. With only a little self-examination we can find out what that is.

HOW DID WE GET OUR STYLE?

Whatever we are at any given time in our life is obviously a product of all that's gone before: all the influences, all the experiences we've had, plus whatever tendencies and traits we may have been born with. As far as our management style is concerned, we acquired it from several sources. First, we do what we do as a result of our history of successes and failures. Successful behaviors have been rewarding, so we're more likely to repeat them. We liked what happened, so we want to see it happen again. When we were confronted with a problem we didn't know how to handle, we screamed at the person bringing the problem, suggesting that the person should have done more work on the problem before bringing it to us. The person left, didn't bother us any more, so we found a way to get rid of bothersome problems. We found this rewarding, so we began to use this course of action. Maybe not all at once, but gradually this behavior seemed to get results we wanted, so we fell into a pattern. The person bringing us the problem had a most unpleasant time of it, though, so he or she is highly unlikely to bring the next problem to us. The next problem may get solved; or it may be solved incorrectly or poorly; or it may not get solved at all. At any rate, it may never get brought to us. But that's only one of the ways we develop a style of management.

Another strong influence on our style are the experiences we've had with other people and their styles, especially our superiors. Without being aware of it, we pick up habits of those who supervise us. This is especially so if we happen to like the person or admire certain characteristics or results obtained. There is also evidence that we pick up the styles of those whom we don't admire or like. We grow accustomed to doing things a certain way because the boss wants us to, and fail to realize that while at one time we didn't approve of this way, it has now become a part of our style. For example, suppose we work for someone who gives us orders to "Go tell them we want it right now and we won't take no for an answer!" Although we may certainly hate doing things in this manner, before long we see that it gets results and we begin to find that it isn't so hard after all. Without meaning to, we've begun to develop a style like that of the person we really didn't like—a style we thought was very bad!

Another reason we tend to pick up the style of the persons we work for is that they're generally the ones who do the appraisals, and we want to please them. Most often, the things they see as bad in us are the things we aren't doing as they would do, and the things they like about us are the things we are doing as they would. The natural consequence is to become more and more like them, all the time saying to ourselves, "If I ever get out from under this person, I'll be quite different," but failing to let the difference show up when that time comes.

Our peers also have a strong influence on our developing style. This is not so much a matter of peer pressure, where our peers demand our conformity. It's more a matter of our *needing* a style in order to say what we've done in certain situations, or what we would have done "if it had been us." When we get into a discussion about problems—whether on coffee break or in the lounge or in the carpool going home—we like to have an answer not only to *how* we plan to handle the situation, but also *why*. That's where the style comes in: "I'm just going to have to do what I always do in situations like this." Of course, we are also influenced by how our peers handle problems. When we have a similar problem, we tend to do what we've seen others do, so we begin to adopt and adapt the styles of other people. There's nothing necessarily wrong with this approach, by the way, especially if we can use the newly acquired style. However, just because something seems to work for someone else does not necessarily mean it will work for us. We may not know the whole story of the other person's problem, which may be different enough from ours to make the approach inappropriate for us. If we try the approach and it doesn't work, we may feel it's our own fault and lose even more confidence in our own ability to establish a style.

Developing a usable style is a slow process at best. Style develops as a result of trial and error, reinforcement or punishment, as we've already seen. But mostly, style develops without much planning. We don't plan to be dictatorial, or wishy-washy, or a good or bad guy. We don't plan to procrastinate in giving decisions when we're asked for them. All these things just sort of happen. The process of developing a style usually comes about like this: we're put into a job as a manager or supervisor. We've had very little training for the job. We get a few suggestions from the boss, a word or two of caution from our peers, then go to it. We aren't completely stupid, so we use our common sense and manage to get by for a few days, then a few weeks, then for a year or so. We may get some words of wisdom from our supervisor at appraisal time. We may finally even get to go to a class or two on how to handle the job. But we're really only doing what comes naturally. We want to please our boss and to get along with the employees we supervise. Putting this all together, we usually end up with a "style" we can call our own. We aren't exactly sure what it is or where it came from, but we have it nevertheless.

Having mentioned training, we should point out that some of our style comes from formal training, while other parts of it come from informal studying on our own. When we go to a class on management, we find ourselves working on cases that may look like the cases we deal with back home—and the more they do look like the cases back home, the more likely we will be to transfer the training back to the real world. We may see some role-playing of situations we can identify with. At lunch, or at night, we may talk to people who have had similar problems and find out some new things to try. Studying on our own, we may read about some new approach. Even in our appraisals we may see and hear things that had never occurred to us. For example, our boss may tell us that we've let our people miss production schedules almost every month, and suggest that there needs to be some sharing of information about these "misses" with the people under us. The fact that the boss even knew about the schedules may shock us, but it may also start us thinking and end up being good training for us. Whatever the case may be, though, we do finally develop some kind of style that is peculiar to us. We may not know where it came from but we use it every day. The question we have to keep asking, however, is not "Where did it come from?" but "Is it the right style for me and my situation?"

HAVE STYLES CHANGED?

Some people have the idea that management styles really haven't changed all that much over the years. In a way this is true. The same styles are around. People are still doing things right and wrong, well and poorly. People are still managing "by the seat of their pants," and people are still managing by delegating and by not delegating, just as they always have. The variety is still there, but hopefully there are more people doing a better job of managing than ever before. The important thing about styles changing, though, is that it creates more alternatives and better understanding of these alternatives. In other words, we *know* more about managing people than we used to, even if we aren't *doing* a much better job of managing. One of the sig-

"Son, remember this—some people think managing is just a matter of 'horse sense' until they don't win, place, or show."

nificant things about management today is that we know enough to see that what we used to do was wrong. We can at least see why some of the things we tried to do failed. As we understand more and more about people, and get a better handle on how people respond and why, we are better able to know how to treat them.

What we have today are new philosophies. We can't really say that we have all the answers, of course, since obviously we don't. We can't say that what we're doing is without question. We have to admit that one day we'll look again at what we're saying and doing right now and realize how little we really knew. But however little we know and however wrong our philosophies are, we're better off now than we used to be. More studies have been made, more people have been looked at under many more circumstances, and more things have been tried with more knowledge of the results. We know more about people's reasons for acting the way they do, and we know more about how to modify the undesirable behaviors and encourage and reinforce the desirable behaviors. But we still have a long way to go in training supervisors in how to use this information—this is why books like this are prepared and presented to people who have been around long enough to appreciate the need for keeping up to date.

Styles are not the only things that have changed. People have changed as well—not basic human nature, fortunately, or we'd never be able to deal with people in any kind of sensible way. The things that have changed about people are their wants, needs, and desires. Later in this chapter we'll see how these changes affect us as supervisors. Even our own styles have changed along the way, if we stop and think about it. Things that bother us now used not to bother us when we were first made supervisors. For example, perhaps it bothers us considerably when we see money being wasted, people misusing their time, or people coming in late for work. At one time we may have had so much on our minds that we didn't give this much thought. On the other hand, we may have too much on our minds to worry about these things now. We may be so engrossed in the problems of our own jobs that we overlook such things.

ARE STYLES ANY BETTER?

As we think about the new philosophies, we can't help but ask ourselves, "Are we really doing any better than we used to do?" That's a pretty easy question to avoid, since we see the same problems around that have always been around. If we're so much better, how come the problems haven't disappeared? How come we still have to worry about money and waste and tardiness? The answer to this really goes back to the question of changing philosophies. It is true that over the years we've been through a number of different philosophies about how to manage people and how to get them to perform as we would like. There's no doubt but what we'll go through some more. But we will never find that we've gone full circle back to where we were at an earlier point in time. We'll never return to "those old days," whenever and whatever they were. Some day this very book will be a classic of error, unless it's revised. Even if it is revised periodically, it will still become out of date just as we do. But we will never pick up this edition and say, "Look at this. This used to be in style—now it's back again," because there will always be additional knowledge. As long as we continue to study human behavior, we'll learn more and more about people and how to deal with their problems. It's true that some things we suggest in this book may not work in certain current circumstances but will work later on, but that's because we don't yet know enough to make them work. Later on we might know enough to handle the right action in the right circumstance.

(Let's pause here to point out parenthetically that we aren't trying to make this book obsolete before it's ever used! Hopefully the reader can see that all we can ever hope to do is the best we know at the time. As we look back at some of the early automobiles or airplanes, we find them rather amusing and wonder how we could have been so backward. At that time, however, we would have thought of these things as being the very latest—*and they were.* So it is with any book dealing with human behavior and the managing of that behavior. If we can keep up with the technology, that's the best we can do. We ought to be glad when we're that far along, rather than moan because we're going to have to change some day.)

Let's look at some reasons why styles of management are better today than ever before. First of all, we know more about performance. The average supervisor knows more about how to set standards for the jobs being supervised. Most experienced supervisors now ask themselves frequently, "Just what is a satisfactory job?" That question—or at least the answer—wouldn't have had nearly as much meaning 20 or 25 years ago. Supervisors know that in order for a person to live up to a standard, there must first *be* a standard. There must be something concrete in the way of performance criteria that is undertandable by the people doing the work. Furthermore, these supervisors know that the standards must be known *and understood* by the workers.

Second, management styles are better because we know a lot more about how to evaluate the performances of the people doing the work. No longer is appraisal time one of nebulous wondering and speculation. Supervisors who have set standards have something to evaluate the employees against, and can therefore evaluate them much more completely. This makes their job much easier, because now they can say, "Here's what you were supposed to do and here's what you did—the difference is the deficiency." Since the employees knew from the beginning what the standards and expectations were, they should not be surprised at appraisal time.

Third, management styles are better because we know more about how to *train* people—and are doing more and better training—than before. When you put all this together, it makes for a great success story. There is a standard of performance that everyone can understand; no one is asked to do anything that is a mystery. Then we know more about how to evaluate performance, so we can tell how well people are doing. Most exciting of all, we know how to train people so they can meet these standards! Not only do people know *what* they're supposed to do, they know *how* they're supposed to do it. So we are doing a better job of managing because we know more about performance and the things related to performance.

We also know more about motivation, and that also makes us better managers of people. We know what turns people on and what turns them off. As we'll see in the chapter on motivation, we've found that people are turned on by some things, but turned off by the absence or presence of quite different things. Motivators and nonmotivators aren't opposites of each other. Bad working conditions demotivate people, but good working conditions don't necessarily cause people to go all out to perform all the time they're on the job. There was a time when we couldn't make this distinction—now that we can, we can be better managers.

Not only do we know more about performance and motivation, but we also know alot more about the factors and compete for the worker's time, interest, and effort. We understand what part community interests play in keeping the employee's ego built up. We can appreciate that many employees have community interests or social goals that aren't in any way related to the organizations they work for. There was a time when we thought the employee owed complete allegiance to the employing organization, 24 hours a day. We've grown a lot smarter now and realize that home, family, community, and recreation are going to command a fair share of the employee's time, energy, and interest; if we're able, we'll try to make this work in our favor rather than against us. At least we realize it's worth a try.

Finally, we're better with our managing styles because we know more about how to integrate the work and the individual into a meaningful relationship. It's more than just matching the worker and the job. It's a matter of fitting goals, personalities, abilities, and attitudes together with mutually agreed-upon objectives.

We should point out here that just because we're a lot better informed than we used to be—just because we're able to do a better job of managing now than a few years ago—we are far from perfect! We've got a long way to go yet, and we have to use our experience and knowledge—and use them wisely—to help us along the way.

THE CHANGING WORK FORCE

One hears frequently about the "good old days" when managing people was pretty simple. There's little evidence to support the fact that managing people was all that simple, but that's not the issue now. The simplicity or lack of it 50 years ago is irrelevant in this age. Whatever else we can say about the days gone by, we can say for certain that *those days will never be back again.* There's no use even speculating about how good or bad the days were (although it will help us to look back at the people and their needs of a few decades ago to see how the work force has changed over the years). The important point is that these days will never come back because things have changed. We have already seen how additional knowledge has altered and will continue to alter management styles. Now let's look at some other forces of change.

For example, people are different from the way they used to be. They want more now because they've seen other people with more. Their aspirations are higher. When they see the possibility of getting more, they raise their sights. Several years ago while traveling through an underdeveloped country and seeing several young boys herding water buffalo, this author asked the driver, a native himself, what the boys wanted to be when they grew up. Did they want to be astronauts, firemen, racing car drivers, or what? The driver thought about the question for a long time and then came up with an answer that clearly explains what we're saying here.

"They don't want to be anything—they don't *know* anything to be!" When one thinks about life without schooling, television, or books—without even the *ability* to read books and newspapers and magazines—it's easy to see the truth of such an answer. But look at our own workers today. Think how much better informed they are than those uninformed boys, and have been all their lives. And think how much better informed they are than workers of 40 years ago. We can see this just looking at the surroundings of their jobs. The training and other efforts at dissemination of information are quicker and more accurate. It's not considered unusual today for the head of an organization to appear on live, closed-circuit television, with monitors placed around the work areas. Even two-way communications can be set up where employees can respond and get answers to questions right at the work site.

People are also much better informed outside of the work environment. Young people graduating from high school today are in many ways more advanced than college graduates of several years ago, at least in terms of the variety of material covered. There are those who are quick to point out that education seems to have deteriorated. "Why, we have people graduating from school who can barely read and write!" While this may be true—and certainly is in a number of cases—there is something quite vital being overlooked: where would these same people have been 40 years ago? Look at the percentage of people graduating from high school and college today as compared to a few years ago, and it's easy to see that these "nonreaders, nonwriters" wouldn't have even thought of staying in school as long as they do today. Good or bad, at least these people have *seen* more books and more teachers than their counterparts of years ago. They've been exposed to educated people and they've been in the same classrooms with those who could read and write. write. They've heard conversations about careers and more education and what the opportunities are "out there" in the world of business. And all of that comes down to the fact that present-day workers are better informed than workers have ever been.

The *speed* with which the workers get their information today is also a factor in the difference between today's employees and those of 40 years ago. We've already mentioned closed-circuit television. Public (home) television is working to change our employees, too. There was a time when battles could be fought after treaties had been signed, when it took days, or at least hours, for people to find out about world-shaking events. Now we live in an age where a leader can be assassinated *while people watch on television.* Instant replays make the news even more present. One of the side effects of such instant information is that it makes people more conscious of the world around them. They don't have to wait to go to a movie and see a newsreel of last week's flood, or last year's drought and accompanying famine. They can see it today while it's happening today. All of this makes them identify with these things much more closely. We're seeing workers with us now who care about things in different ways than ever before, and much of the reason is the speed with which they get informed.

We'll never go back to the old days because *organizations have changed* as well. Hiring policies are different now than they used to be. In many ways, there is a paradox with regard to hiring policies. On the one hand we have seen the employment of many more technical individuals who can understand and use complex machines like the computer, while on the other hand we've seen the employment of relatively low-skilled people to do the mundane, uncomplicated work associated with this complex equipment. Less-qualified workers have been hired because of social conscience, government requirements, or both, which has forced us to learn more about training—and once having learned, we will continue to train from now on. One reason we can't stop our training is that the same conscience or force that started us hiring less-skilled people has also caused us to think in terms of "upward mobility." We've found that it's not enough to leave our people in entrance jobs; we must provide for their movement up to better jobs. This means more and better training. And since our understanding of performance is better, we know that we can no longer just "expose" people to training. We have to provide training that is realistic and produces results. Like it or not, this is a decided change over some years ago.

Another irony of our present-day world is that although we've learned a lot about people, we have at the same time become *machine oriented* in our thinking. We have more people working today than ever before, but as we'll see we aren't using their talents very well in many cases. We have people who are better informed, better educated, and who have a desire to move up, but we are giving them very menial jobs. There was a time when we considered janitorial work as "menial," which it is, but we now find that we've created menial tasks in many other locations. In the computer rooms around the country we've got people doing punch-card work and assorting work that requires little or no skill at all. In many cases we've automated jobs almost beyond the need for human activity, *but not quite.* At one time the workers made "whole" decisions, not partial or small ones. Now they often don't even know where the work comes from or where it's going. They're almost machines themselves. When it comes to motivation, this has had disastrous results.

Another reason we won't go back to the old days is that

workers have changed their viewpoint toward the organizations they work for. There are strong rights movements in most organizations, and in the others the people are at least thinking about their rights and how they can get them. And people's definition of "rights" is quite different from what it used to be. Because of the outside ideas they have been exposed to, people think it quite appropriate to stand up to management where they wouldn't have done so in the past. Perhaps affluence has given them courage, but whatever the reason, workers rarely feel that they are bought and paid for by management so must do management's bidding. People who have never experienced a massive work shortage such as existed in the depression years aren't likely to feel too dependent on those who give them jobs—even though the ones offering the jobs may have a different attitude.

In addition to the rights movement, which has caused people to demand more and to demand more loudly, the welfare system of the country has perhaps made it possible for people to feel more independent, as have the unemployment compensation systems. (Incidentally, this isn't intended as an attack on workers who are demanding their rights or who are on unemployment. It's just an effort to point out the nature of present-day workers, and to show how they differ from workers in the past.)

Another change in the viewpoint of the workers is that many of the younger workers *apparently* have different goals than those who went to work a generation or two ago. (We have to say "apparently," since only time will tell what the result will be.) They seem to be vocalizing their feelings in pretty loud ways, and if we are hearing correctly, they're saying that they see the world as a unit, of which their jobs, the organization, and the community are all integral parts. Few of them seem willing to separate themselves from the world for eight hours a day, to return to it only at quitting time. They see the problems of starvation, or pollution, or energy conservation as being related to the job and the organization as well as the community. They have a much keener sense of hypocrisy, and the younger workers particularly won't stand still for very long in what they think is a hypocritical situation. Again, though, let's point out that it's not a question of whether or not it *really is* hypocrisy; the point is that as long as it's *perceived* as hypocrisy, they will react against it. Only time will tell whether they will learn to live with hypocrisy and deal with it as others have done; whether they will be able to institute enough changes to do away with hypocrisy; or whether they will realize that what they see as hypocrisy isn't always that.

What we have come down to is that for whatever reason, today's workers no longer see the organization as "infallible," and hence are not as dependent on it as some have been in the past. This means we aren't likely to go back to the old ways of managing people, be they simple ways or not. Interestingly enough, historically, organizations have tended to lag behind the workers by ten to 15 years in terms of keeping up with changes. Perhaps it takes this long for the truth to surface in a recognizable fashion. Whatever the reason, it means that the supervisor must be constantly aware that people do change, and that no matter how much we learn about people, *they may be one jump ahead of us.*

MATCHING SKILLS WITH STYLE

We need to go back to something we said earlier—that management is a skill, or series of skills. (Whether we call it "managing" or "supervising," the same holds true: both are skills.) *Skills have to be learned.* Skills can be done well, poorly, or in between. As we learn a management skill well, we can use it and it becomes part of our "style." As we develop this skill—be it writing, running a meeting, delegating work, whatever—as soon as it becomes easy and natural for us to use it, it becomes part of our style. As our style changes, we need to evaluate the results of these changes to see if we're getting what we want. What we need are frequent self-evaluations to see what our strengths are. A good self-evaluation includes looking at our problems as well as our performance. Do we have problem employees we didn't used to have? Do we find it more difficult to deal with unruly employees than we used to? Do we find ourselves in trouble with our bosses more often than usual? These kinds of questions will tell us if we're changing for the worse.

What we need to find out is whether we are using our strengths or stumbling over our weaknesses. Good supervisor/managers will quickly identify strengths and weaknesses and do two things with what they find. First, they will work very hard at strengthening these areas of weakness, and second, they will try to delegate as much work as possible to those who are stronger in these areas. If conducting meetings is easy for us, we will conduct the meetings, but if we find writing letters difficult, we get those who work for us who are better at writing letters to write them for us, while we try to figure out how we can improve in this area. We need to ask ourselves if we have skills—either new or old—that we aren't using. We need to ask ourselves if there are new skills we have to learn, perhaps because of job changes. If we continue to ask these kinds of questions, we'll keep ourselves developing. We'll not only end up doing a better job on the present assignment, but we'll also find ourselves qualified for other, more responsible jobs.

CONCLUSION

When all is said and done, we must realize that whether we know it or not, whether it's good or bad, *we all have a style of managing*. If we don't even think about our style, we still have one. If we have very few strengths, then our style is a weak management style, but nevertheless a style. If we are indecisive, then we have an indecisive style. If we are autocratic because we're afraid to delegate, then we have an autocratic style. If we change from day to day, or from week to week, sometimes being firm, sometimes being soft, then our style is one that is frustrating to our subordinates, but nevertheless a style. We have developed our style in strange ways. We may have gotten it from former bosses, from reading books, from trial and error, from reasoning things out—but wherever we got it, it is ours until we change it. We may need to change it, too. We find that out by examining our actions and the results of these actions. Not just once but over a period of time. Even if we are satisfied with our style, we need to be constantly aware that people, organizations, and viewpoints change. And therefore we too may have to change. We change to meet new challenges of the job. We change to meet new attitudes of the employees and higher management. We need to be flexible to meet the situations we find ourselves in to the best of our ability. More than this, though, we need to grow and develop to be ready to move on to the next challenge. If we're doing our job of developing ourselves into a person with a good style of managing other people, then when it comes time to move to another job, we won't think of it as running away from a miserable assignment; we'll think of it as moving on to a bigger and better challenge, as well as a more exciting job.

DISCUSSION ACTIVITIES

1. Give a simple, reasonably complete definition of "management style." Write down a description of your own style of management. 49

2. What are the influences on us as we develop a style of managing? 50, 51, 52

3. Why is it a management style can feel *comfortable* or *uncomfortable* to us? Pg 63

4. Discuss the possibility that a management style can feel comfortable to us and still be inappropriate for our managing situation. 64

5. Discuss (debate) this statement: "If a management style is comfortable for us it is better to use it than move to one that is uncomfortable for us." Pg 64

6. What are the possibilities of a style being correct in a particular situation, then becoming the wrong one over a period of time in that *same* situation? Pg 55 + 57 56

7. List as many ways as possible in which workers hired today will differ from those hired 25 years ago. Ten years ago. Ten years from now. 58- 63

chapter 5

MOTIVATING—CAN IT BE DONE?

Among supervisors both old and young there are skeptics who would question our ability to motivate people to either work harder, enjoy their work, appreciate the organization's problems, or want to help others out with their work. They would say, with emphasis, "No, you can't motivate people, in spite of all the things that have been said and written about the subject!" The truth is, though, it *is* possible to motivate people to do most of these things. Facts show that people *can* be changed to where they really do show interest, and even pride, in their work. Admittedly, we probably can't motivate them as well as some would have us believe. Some would have us think there is nothing that can't be accomplished through certain motivational efforts. Here the facts are against them. However, it is possible to motivate people better than most of us think. Just how much can we motivate people? How can we be sure we're doing the right thing to motivate them? Just how much effort will it take and how much effort is it worth?

Much has been written and said about motivation. More has been said about it than done about it, leaving a lot of mileage in the statement, "After all is said and done, more will be *said than done!*" There has been some pretty good research on the subject, however, so in this chapter we'll try to cover the things that we really do know for sure about motivating people. We'll look at the problems, see what causes many of them, and learn not only how we can solve these problems but also how we can avoid them in the future. We'll discover that much of what is known on the subject isn't all that new, and perhaps we've just failed to listen. Finally, we'll discuss the most important thing of all: How do we motivate our people?

A UNIVERSAL TOPIC

Research people have studied motivation for a long time. They have looked at it under almost every condition imaginable, in almost every kind of job situation, and in almost every country that reports on this kind of research. The reason is simple: it's a universal problem. Apparently we're destined to continue to talk about motivation for a long time to come, because (as we have seen and will see further in this chapter) people change from one era to another. This means that what works in one era may not do the complete job in the next era. It also suggests that we haven't found the complete answer to the problem yet, so we have to keep trying.

One problem we have in discussing motivation is that it is a much misunderstood subject. Let's see just what we're talking about when we discuss "motivation." When we talk about the process of motivating others, all too often we get the feeling that motivating someone is something to do "externally" to produce harder-working, more loyal people. This is not exactly right. Motivation, in the true sense, comes from within the person. In other words, our actions create an environment that allows the person to become motivated. This newly created environment isn't all that tangible, of course—it involves perhaps a different kind of responsibility, a different look at the job, a different feeling about the importance of the assignment, or whatever. The point is that we see a change in the behavior of the individual because the environment is different from the previous one, which wasn't motivating the employee. (This is not a point to get overly concerned about. Some have debated it for years, though it doesn't warrant that much attention. We'll be content to live with those who argue that if we change the environment, which we control, then we are motivating the employee. Whether it's internal or external doesn't really matter if the end results suit our goals.)

Do we know enough about motivation to change people's

performance? Can we get them motivated? Can we alter the environment enough to cause a person to work (think) differently? Yes—we definitely know enough about people's work habits, their desires, and their reactions to various situations to install good conditions for motivation. The studies that have been made are *sound*. The data are substantial, factual, usable, and adaptable. It shall not be our purpose to go into these studies in any depth, nor to try to prove them. We'll try only to see how we can apply what the studies have shown us. The successful application of these things will be proof enough to those who use the information. If the application is unsuccessful, then that too will teach us something.

WHY MOTIVATION PROBLEMS?

As we've already said, we've always had motivation problems, and will continue to have them in the future. Is this because we haven't succeeded in solving the problems, or is there some other reason? We've suggested earlier in this chapter that the answer is that people and organizations are always changing. Let's go into this in more detail.

If we look back to the days of the Great Depression, we'll see that though people were glad to have jobs, there were still problems with motivation. Studies during that time and before on the attitudes of the workers revealed that people then wanted to be recognized as individuals, to be something other than a part of an assembly line or one more piece of machinery. And they would work harder in exchange for this proper recognition of them as people. Later, after World War II, people began to see things differently. They still wanted the recognition, but they wanted something more substantial in addition—they wanted benefits, better wages, and tangible rewards. In the thirties there had been little time for *constant* recreation, like boating every weekend for several months out of the year. Working days were longer, and the working week was often five and a half to six days long. There was less mobility. People tended to take only one big trip a year, and it was only for a week or two. But by the forties and fifties, there was increasing demand for shorter working hours. People began to demand and to take longer vacations. The war had introduced people to different parts of the country. Soldiers returning home thought less about moving around, and there was even a hint of restlessness. But it's hard to take longer vacations, longer weekends, and longer trips without the money and means to do so. All of this was reflected in the demands for and the subsequent granting of higher wages and better benefits, including more vacations and holidays.

In the sixties and seventies people took a serious look at education, and it was improved. It was not only better—it was better for *more people*. And we became a more informed nation, not solely as a result of more meaningful, intentional education. Our communications devices were improved to the point that very few things could happen anywhere in the world without their being heard of (and seen in many cases) right in the living room of the average home. While schools have yet to cope with the explosion of knowledge in the proper depth, at least today's average high-school graduate has been exposed to a much greater variety of things than the graduate of a few decades earlier. Now, what has all this got to do with what workers are telling us today? Simply that the average workers are better informed and better able to do most jobs today than they were a few years ago.

A look at many of the jobs, though, should cause us to stop and wonder if all this ability is necessary. While jobs are being done on more complex systems than ever before, the actual mental and physical requirements are often quite below what they used to be. The truth is, workers in the sixties and seventies find themselves better qualified to do more meaningful tasks, but often are asked to do much less meaningful tasks than their parents and grandparents. Of even more significance is the fact that the one thing that could have made this all right—*job responsibility*—is missing. Workers in assembly lines are unaware of where things are coming from to get to this work station, or where things are going when they leave the station. Big corporations decentralize and dissipate the work to such a degree that only the very top people can actually claim any real responsibility for meaningful decisions. This lack of responsibility is causing the workers to begin to tell us something else: "Keep on with your recognition; keep on treating us well; but, please, *use us well!*"

Most current motivation programs, therefore, are aimed at finding a way to give the workers meaningful, responsible jobs, as much as they are able to take. The process is called *job enrichment*. We'll see how it works later in this chapter.

WHERE ARE WE GOING FROM HERE?

It may be useless to speculate on what the workers will be saying to us a few years from now, but there are some signs that might alert us to what to expect. Workers have become more involved in social change, more concerned with the world around them, more active in community affairs, and this new emphasis is reflected on the job. Workers now often worry about pollution. They are concerned about the air, the water, the noise, the wildlife, and the soil. We have to realize, too, that this isn't just a passing fancy—it's a real worry. People have had these concerns for several years by the time they come on the payroll, and they come from a group that has been able to make enough waves to get something done. They have seen the power of getting together and standing for a cause. They have seen the results of such action, which has been *visible change*. What this may well mean for the supervisor is that these people may have less loyalty to the organization, and more loyalty to the world around them—in fact, they may well feel that the world around them is *more* important than the organization. If this were true of just a few people, it wouldn't be worth discussing in this book. But since it represents a generation or two, it is important that the supervisor understand the reason for some of the actions and attitudes to be encountered as a result.

First, workers will be less inclined to do things unless there is a good reason—better, for example, than "organizational policy." This is going to go down hard with older, experienced supervisors who are used to doing things just because the boss said to, whether they like it or not. In fact, most supervisors aren't going to take to giving explanations for every action. But we're going to see later on that this isn't such a bad idea—from an entirely different point of view. When we get to talking about managing a group by objectives—that is, setting goals *with the help of the employees*—we'll see that the employees will work better and perform better under these conditions. For now, though, let's just say that this is one of the things we can expect from the new employees hired in the seventies.

Next, workers will be less inclined to simply accept us as their boss. Not that there's anything wrong with us, or that they feel they're "better"—they just won't have the same feeling about calling someone a "superior" and themselves "subordinates." (Remember, they've spent a lot of time working for equality before joining the organization.) Will it be impossible to deal with this kind of thinking? Is it all wrong, and are we going to have to "straighten them out"? No, to both of these questions. It won't be impossible to deal with this attitude and we will more likely be the ones to get straightened out than them. This attitude doesn't mean that these people cannot or will not accept supervision, nor that they think they're too good to be supervised. It does mean, however, they they will question some of the things we never questioned, at least out loud. In many ways, they're just like us in their thinking: they question the same seemingly idiotic policies; they question the "hurry up so we can wait" activities; they question the inefficiencies we have questioned; and they question some of the hypocritical actions we perhaps may not have thought of quite that way, but some that we've questioned too. The difference isn't in what they question, rather in the *way* they question. They will be and already are more vocal. They won't feel the restrictions and inhibitions we feel about speaking out against the organization or the boss or the folks upstairs.

Another new thing we can expect from workers in the seventies and eighties is that they were raised in relative affluence, so that they will worry less about losing their jobs. While we have seldom used the threat of firing to control the workers, it was nevertheless one of the options available to us. There are workers who've been around awhile who still worry about being laid off, even some of those who are protected fairly well by union agreements. Members of the newer generation not only won't feel too strongly about losing their jobs, they may actually expect to change jobs as they go along. The change may be for variety. It may be because they develop more skills, or different skills. It may be because they don't like working for our organization. They won't necessarily leave for more money; some may leave for less, if they find a job they think they'll like better.

WHAT MOTIVATES PEOPLE?

How do we handle these employees? Is it possible to motivate them and get productive work out of them? Certainly. In fact, *productive work* may well be the best answer we can find to motivate them. Remember, we said earlier in this chapter that workers today are telling us that they want to be *used well*. This isn't just the *new* worker. This is most of the work force. This isn't just the salaried worker or the hourly paid worker, either. It's everyone, in every kind of job, at all levels. While there are exceptions, the general rule is that most people today like to think they're doing something worthwhile. But before we go into this, let's see some things that affect motivation, other than just what people are saying to us.

We've talked about changes in people and organizations. These affect motivation, as do managerial approaches. We have new managers using old ways of supervising. The new people supervise as they were supervised—if they were supervised poorly, they will carry this bad supervision on to another generation. We have the same old supervisors supervising in the same old bad ways, and when the workers see other, good supervisors, they are affected by the difference. They wonder why they should be so unlucky. Then we have organizations with cloudy goals. The goals never seem to come quite into focus, and even when they do, they change frequently. Just about the time people think they have a handle on what's going on, the objectives or the emphasis seem to change to something else. Perhaps there is an austerity program and all the workers are told to cut back on expenditures, save on materials, reuse paper and other expendable items, pick up paperclips, and not expect increased wages. Then about the time they've adjusted to this, they find the organization has just decided to renovate the offices, or build a new building, or buy new office furniture—something that doesn't seem to be a necessity. This can have a devastating effect on motivation.

On the other hand, people may get used to good times—

times when there is plenty of money available, a high budget, few restrictions, and not very close scrutiny on how the money is spent. Then comes a recession and expenditures are suddenly watched very closely. Every penny has to be accounted for. Things that were once taken for granted as necessities are cut out. Half-finished projects are abandoned or postponed. Pet projects are eliminated. The work force is cut back through attrition. No new employees are brought in. The shock of such things will also have a large effect on motivation, especially if they aren't managed very carefully.

But we aren't really talking about these drastic changes, nor are we talking about poorly run organizations with fuzzy goals. We're talking about normal times where there is some, but not much, fluctuation in the budget, in numbers of people, or in policies. What is it that motivates people during these kinds of times? What do we know for sure?

WHAT WE KNOW FOR SURE

Although people change with respect to what's important to them, what they expect to get out of life, and their feelings about the organization, *they don't change in basic human nature.* For this we can be glad, because we can study people in depth and apply what we find out at any time to most people, most any place, doing most any kind of job. We depend on human nature not changing. The process of figuring out how to motivate our people is to learn some facts about human nature, find out how our people fit into the picture, and then apply what we have learned to the people we are supervising.

Let's see what all that means. First, it's necessary to review Maslow's hierarchy of needs in a simplified way. This will help us determine what kinds of needs a person has so we can see how to fulfill these needs. Maslow's theory (which is pretty well documented as accurate) is that people do things because they have certain needs. These needs differ from one person to another because different people have already met different needs— some have already moved higher up the "needs ladder" than others. The important thing to remember is that when one need is satisfied, we go to the next one, *but not before.*

Physical Needs

At the bottom of the ladder—if we may oversimplify—are the physical needs, with food, clothing, and shelter coming first. We rarely would think about solving social problems in our lives if we didn't know where the next meal was coming from. We would hardly worry about not fulfilling our potential when we were without even a place to sleep at night. In fact, if we were starving for food or dying of thirst in the hot desert, we'd risk going to a pond with a few snakes around it if we could just get to the water.

Safety Needs

On the other hand, if we were merely out for a drive in an air-conditioned car and stopped by the side of the road to walk in the sand, we wouldn't go near such a pond if we even suspected snakes might be around. With the "survival" or physical need met, we start to worry about safety. This moves us up the ladder, since we develop the safety need only after we have the first step cared for.

Psychological Needs

From here we get into the psychological needs. First, we need to be accepted as a person, to be liked, to belong to some group or have somebody who wants us around just for who we are. This is our *social* need. As Maslow saw it, this social need was essentially one of being loved by someone close to us and feeling as if we belonged to someone we could get close to. Mostly this need is met by the family, but if the worker's need isn't met at home, it gets brought to the office or other work location. Most of us have known older, frequently unmarried, workers who take a parental attitude toward the new employees. As these new employees come along, often right out of high school, the older worker will fuss over them, help them get started, answer all their questions, and generally show a great deal of tenderness toward them. While we certainly wouldn't want to impugn anyone's motives, nor suggest that this is the only reason that this kind of activity takes place, seeking after love and belonging is nevertheless one reason why people do these kinds of things. They simply haven't been able to get their need for belonging met elsewhere, so they do it on the job. Not that there is anything wrong with this. It's a function that needs to be taken care of in most work places, so we should be glad when it's done, and not care why nor even look for a motive. However, if it begins to interfere with the regular work assigned to the person giving out this tenderness, then it does become serious. When we deal with it, we just have to remember to continue to allow for opportunities for this person to be respected and cared about.

As we have said, most people's needs for belonging and being loved are met at home or outside the work place. But there is a higher order of this need that is expressed at the office or in the shop, and that's the need to belong day to day in the work group. Here the experienced supervisor will have to be careful and see that this need is met in the right way. Remember, we tend to overlook faults in people we care for, and when a supervisor overlooks an employee's failure to meet job standards so that the employee won't feel "unwanted," there is a real hazard. Obviously, there is a danger in both directions. If we make the employee feel not wanted, then one of the basic needs isn't getting met and we have a frustrated, unmotivated worker. If we let the worker continue to do bad work, then the job suffers and both the employee and ourselves will have to pay for it in the long run.

Those who have been around for very long will see this need being met in various ways, usually in the form of peer organizing. To some extent, even a carpool fills part of this need. People get together and let another person join the group, be a part of it, and make decisions on what time to leave, who will drive on certain days, which route to take, and so on. We say, "I belong to a carpool," hence showing that this need is being met to a degree, at least. Work groups form bowling teams or other athletic groupings, giving the workers a chance again to belong to something. Work groups get together and form allegiances to certain causes, even against the organization or the boss. Notice that people "belong to the union," but rarely ever use the expression "belong to the company." If they do, it is meant in derision, suggesting they have "sold their souls to the company store"! This concept of belonging to something other than the organization works as a real hardship on the supervisor. In places where there are strong unions, the employees think of the union as getting them whatever they need: they go to the union when they are disciplined and think it was unjust or they go to the union if they don't like what's going on with the boss or the organization. Where there aren't unions, employees become very engrossed in their petty problems and we don't seem to know why. The truth is, they have a need for belonging that isn't being met on the job. They have no one who seems to care about their problems, so their problems loom larger and larger.

What can the supervisor do? Does this mean that we go around and pat everybody on the head and tell them we love them? Do we have birthday parties and group sings every afternoon? Well, all the fun not withstanding, that's not the most effective way of meeting this need. It certainly doesn't do much for the organization, either, at least as far as production is concerned. We have an excellent opportunity to take advantage of this need for being a part of a group—even if there is a strong union. For eight hours a day, give or take a few minutes, we have these employees on the job. We are their supervisor. We represent the organization. We also represent the job itself, since we assign the work and go over the performance with the person. We can make this whole thing a drudgery, and fail completely to meet the belonging need, or we can meet it by doing some team building, as we'll discuss later on. We can create a feeling of being needed on the job by giving recognition to the employee for doing a meaningful job. Some have solved the belonging problems by having an open house on occasions and letting the employees bring their families to the work site. When this has been done, the same thing invariably happens: no matter what else is going on, the workers always head straight for their own work station—be it a typewriter or a boiler—and say, "This is where I work!"

The ideal way to meet the need for acceptance is to have frequent meetings with the people to explain why things are being done the way they are, to explain changes and the reasons for

"Phil, don't you think you've carried this 'home-away-from-home' thing a little too far?"

these changes, to show what progress has been made and what contribution the employees have made toward this progress, and, most importantly, to get the employees' views on what should and could be done in the future. That's what we do when we belong to something—we contribute our energies and our *thoughts* to making a go of it. The wise supervisor will constantly look for ways to let people feel they are contributing to *their* organization. Ironically, every employee *is* a part of the organization, if he or she contributes anything at all toward its well-being. Not only that, but the organization constantly provides evidence that it *wants* the employees to "belong" to it. The organization provides health care, retirement plans, all kinds of benefits—often even profit sharing, which is one of the highest forms of recognition that the employees belong. When these things appear to come as a result of pressure, the employees fail to see the connection and certainly don't get any feeling of belonging. By the same token, if the employees have a strong tie with the job, and feel a part of the work activity as far as planning and goal-setting are concerned, they will naturally react favorably toward any offers the organization makes, and give the organization credit for "caring" about them. Hence their need for belonging will be met.

The Need for Recognition

Let's not forget that once a need is met, people aren't necessarily satisfied—they just develop additional needs. After the physiological, safety, and social needs are fulfilled, therefore, people go a step higher in the hierarchy. They now look for *status or recognition.* Not only do we want to feel we belong to something—that we have a "home," as it were, at the office—but we also have a need to be better than somebody at something. Listen to people talking at coffee break and you can get a good example of this. Whoever went fishing and caught the first fish hasn't got a chance in the fishstory contest. The next person caught one bigger, or has a secret place better than anyone else's, or got more mosquito bites. These are all symptoms of our striving for some recognition. We are trying to meet the need for status. If our time has come for meeting this need (and by the way, most of the people we have working for us have reached this level), then we're going to do so somehow, either on the job or off of it. We'll try to do it on the job, but if everybody there is as good or better than we are, we're not very sure of getting recognition by outworking our co-workers, so we look somewhere else. (Few of our workers *consciously* know that they're looking for this, by the way.) Some workers again turn to the employee organizations for meeting this need. They get recognition by outbowling, or outscoring, or outcrochetting the other workers. Many will soon lose interest in this outside activity if they don't excel in some way, as excelling is their purpose. Often they also lose interest if they begin to get some recognition on the job.

We find that sometimes employees will have to go outside the organization altogether to find their recognition. As long-time supervisors have experienced, sometimes the worker who appears the laziest or least motivated will surprise us by being president of the parent-teachers' association, or a leader in the little league football or baseball organizations. We may discover that this marginal worker we have despaired of making anything out of is, in fact, a leader in the community. This should suggest to us that there is something missing on the job, some recognition that the employee is failing to get, that is being received outside the job. Now let's be sure that we understand what is being said here. We aren't suggesting that there is anything wrong with the employee working in the church or in the community or in the school. Nor are we saying that the only reasons people have for doing these things are to meet needs for recognition or status. We just mean that if the employee isn't performing on the job satisfactorily, this *may* suggest that the job is failing to offer something that is being obtained elsewhere. It also tells us that the employee has some ability that isn't being utilized on the job, whoever is at fault. Successful supervisors have learned to spot these symptoms and take advantage of the knowledge by offering recognition on the job.

The Need to Grow

The highest-order need in the hierarchy is the need to use our talents to the best of our ability. We want a chance to grow as far as we think we can grow. Not only do we want recognition for what we have done, but we want a chance to become even better and use whatever talents we think we have. We don't like to think that anyone or anything is in our way. We don't like the idea that the organization isn't giving us a chance to learn something different or move on to another job, if we think we're able to do that job. Maslow called this the need for "self-actualization." We would like to become what we think we can become. Now this doesn't mean that we actually *can* become these things. We just want the right to find out without the organization interfering with the effort. Remember, though, not everybody has this need all the time. Unless our need for recognition is met, for example, we aren't likely to worry about going on to something bigger and better (except if we think it will get us the recognition we are seeking).

Assuming that this recognition need has been met, what do we do as supervisors to meet the next one that takes over? The selfactualization need isn't an easy need to meet, and if there was ever a time to match the job assignment and the person doing the job, this is it. For instance, if we promote a person to a higher-skilled job before the person has the need to expand, then we'll probably frustrate the person and then be surprised that the person doesn't perform as we'd like. We're surprised because the person was doing so well on the previous job we thought it was a natural move. When we move the person to that more complex job, or even a different or unfamiliar one, we face the danger of causing the person to lose some of the recognition (after the original excitement of the change) or some of the status gained from doing well on the previous job. We're in trouble when we do find ourselves in this situation because the solution isn't to simply move the person back to the old job and say, "Sorry, I thought you could handle that new challenge." Obviously we wouldn't say it like that, but any move back to the old job is going to come out *sounding* like that, regardless of what we say. We've got to pick our changes well, and use the people well in the new jobs, since there is no satisfactory way to cover up a mistake.

Another reason for matching people with the right jobs is that if we have someone who *is* ready to go on—who does have this need—and we don't move that person, then we've got some real motivation problems. Here we have someone who feels ready for a bigger challenge, having met the need for recognition on the existing job, an opening comes up, and the person doesn't get it. Whatever justifiable reasons we may have for not giving that person the job (and there are obviously all kinds), we still have a problem on our hands. We'll have to recognize it before we can deal with it, so let's see how it will manifest itself. If you've been around long as a supervisor, you'll recognize the symptoms. People start to suddenly run the organization down, when they used to be all for it. Policies that never used to bother these people suddenly become major annoyances. Gradually their work slips and they aren't as dependable as before. In the extreme cases, we call these people "bitter." We see ourselves looking at employees we thought had great potential—who were dependable, desirable, and set examples for others—and who now are not only disgruntled and marginal performers, but are also affecting the performance of others and have to be dealt with in a disciplinary way. How did it happen? Was it because we were poor supervisors? Did we make some horrible mistake? No, not really. We probably could have avoided the problem to some extent, but the basic cause was that we had an employee who had reached the highest level of need, and when the opportunity arose for the employee to get the need met (or so it appeared to the employee), it didn't happen.

What do we do in a situation like that? The best thing is to anticipate that it *could* happen. One of the ways of telling whether we're getting better at supervising or just getting more experience at being bad is to see how well we predict behavior. As we gain more experience and learn from that experience, we get to where we can predict the possibility of exactly this kind of thing happening. Just knowing that it might happen will help us a lot. We can take certain action just in case we might have a problem. If we suspect that there is going to be a problem, we can be sure that the employee we are picking for the job—instead of the one who feels he or she is ready—is the best choice. We're in better shape to make the right decision if we go over our reasons for the choice, and weigh all the candidates and the facts again. If this shows that we're right in our choice, then we should still go with it, because our choice must be based on what's best for the organization. We then look at the employee who might have felt equally (or more) qualified. We see what we can do to make his or her *existing* job more challenging. We offer chances for more independent work, more decision making, more chances to experiment, or whatever will make the employee feel that there is still growth possibility in the present job. Don't forget that we're talking about an employee who is already performing above average, who has the recognition and status needs met, and who may eventually go on to a higher or more skilled job. We aren't talking about a substandard employee who is just miffed at not getting a promotion. That's a different world, which we'll talk about in another chapter. By the way, one thing we don't do is go to that employee who is performing well but didn't get the assignment and explain what a great person the employee is who got the job. This will only compound the problem, since all it does is take away from the status rather than solve anything.

FAILING TO GET NEEDS MET—WHAT HAPPENS?

So far we've talked about moving up the scale of needs, pointing out frequently that as one need is met, we move up to a higher-order need. As the survival needs are met, we begin to worry about safety, then we are concerned with being loved and belonging. From there we start having needs for status, for being better than somebody in something. Finally, when all the other needs have been met up to this point, we have a need to grow and become a bigger person, with a chance to show what we can do. But what happens when we reach any of these levels and then, for some reason or another, one of the lower-order needs stops being met? Simple. We just forget where we are and drop back to meet that one. If something happens in our social life that causes us to feel that we are no longer belonging where we want to belong, or that our loved ones are against us or no longer around, then we are apt to worry less about status and more about this need for being loved. If we have had everything going our way, getting plenty of recognition all along, so that we are more concerned with our "self-actualization," and all of a sudden we discover that somebody else is getting credit for something we've done, then we're back down to the recognition need in a hurry. Forget about actualization—who's this getting all the roses for the fine job I did? Who's this taking over some of my job, thinking it can be done better? What do you mean you're taking the sign off the door with my name on it? How come we're no longer getting to sign these worksheets ourselves? In short, we never want to give up one of these areas once we've reached it, and we'll come right back to it with sword in hand if necessary to protect it. As supervisors, we have to remember that, or we'll lose much of the ground we've gained with our employees.

CONCLUSION

So what does all this mean to us as supervisors—this business of levels of needs, and this matter of people wanting to be recognized and treated well and used well? It means that as experienced supervisors, we can't let this information get away from us, even for a day. We have to bear it in mind all the time. We have to use the information to understand our people. After all, our job is to get the job done through other people and the best way to do this is to understand why they act as they do, and why they sometimes even appear irrational. What makes our people so different from us? We act the same way, react to the same things in the same ways, because we have the same needs that must be met in the same ways. Not only will reviewing this kind of information be helpful to us in understanding our people, it will be equally helpful in getting us to understand ourselves. Of course, we have to do some deep self-analysis, and since we don't always like what we see when we look at ourselves, this is awfully hard to do. But we can do it, and should do it, as we'll see in the last chapter.

DISCUSSION ACTIVITIES

1. Discuss (debate) this statement: "We don't know enough about motivation to change people's behavior."

2. List some of the "sacred cows" of management that the newer workers may find as stumbling blocks to motivation.

73-74

3. List characteristics of workers that never seem to change.

4. Discuss (debate) this statement: "Workers today are no longer motivated to do quality work, which is really society's fault." *69- 71 + 72*

5. List ways of giving people recognition and/or status without changing the job or spending money. *— 82*

6. What are some of the symptoms that indicate an employee is not getting enough recognition on the job? *81*

7. List ways in which we take recognition/status away from people, when we're really trying to do something good for the people or the organization as a whole. *80*

chapter 6
MOTIVATING BY JOB ENRICHMENT

In the preceding chapter we talked about motivation in terms of how people have changed and what we know for sure about people. The idea was to show that the more we know about people—including ourselves—the easier it is to get them to perform satisfactorily on the job. We saw that people have different needs at different times, and that our job as supervisor is to find these needs and try to meet them on the job, *with the job.* In this chapter we want to talk about internal and external motivation, and we will hopefully define those terms in meaningful ways. We want to learn about more of the things we know for sure about people—what satisfies them and what dissatisfies them—and how we can use this information to our advantage as supervisors. Experienced supervisors will recognize the truth in the things we say and be able to relate to the examples, even finding examples of their own in most cases.

EXTERNAL VERSUS INTERNAL MOTIVATION

As we mentioned in the preceding chapter, there are those who say that it is impossible for one person to motivate another. They reason that motivation is inside the person, and has to come from within. All we do, they argue, is provide an environment in which they may or may not motivate themselves to do something. Frankly, this is something like the old chicken and egg quarrel, and we don't intend to settle that right here (or anywhere else, for that matter). What we do want to talk about is that different forces cause people to do things; sometimes these forces come from outside a person, sometimes they come from within. Those forces from outside we'll call "external" motivators. These are things that somebody else does to a person to get things done, so in our context they are things that somebody other than the worker does to get *that* worker to do the job. "Internal" motivators, on the other hand, will be defined as those things initiated by the worker without any external actions by others. This sounds too complicated to make much sense, so let's settle it by looking at some examples.

For example, if we threaten an employee with drastic action unless a task is performed in a certain way, then stand by and watch the employee perform, any motivation is obviously *external*. On the other hand, if the employee does a job because it is pleasing in some way, the motivation is internal. Don't let the word "pleasing" fool you, though, because we aren't talking just about pleasant tasks where the weather is fine, the load is light, and everybody is happy. We could be talking about a very difficult job, one that took a long time to accomplish under difficult circumstances. We've all had jobs like that, which actually were very satisfying when they were done. We could be proud of our accomplishment, or people were amazed that we could work under those conditions, or it was a job that we had designed—all those things may have made it "pleasing."

We don't want to give the idea that all external motivation is bad, by the way. And even threats may be necessary at times, though hopefully seldom. But there are other kinds of external motivation, by our definition. Sometimes empolyees do something just to please us, just because they think we would like it. They like us, or respect us, and don't want us to think that they don't want to do a good job. They don't like to see us unhappy, so they perform well on the job. We can't help but be satisfied when that happens. The resulting job is usually very good, and if we're wise we'll show our appreciation. There is a problem with this kind of motivation, though, and we should notice it here. Since it is external (the force being us) it has some of the same drawbacks as the threats we mentioned earlier. Just as when we threaten an employee, the employee who wants to please us is in a dilemma when we're not there. The threatened employee may just goof off until we show up, then go hard at it again. If the acting boss doesn't threaten with the same dire consequences, the employee may not even work hard in the presence of the substitute boss. The same is true with the employees who want to please us. When we're gone they may not like the replacement boss, may not want to be as satisfying, may not have the same respect, so they don't do as good a job as when we're there. If for some reason we're moved on to some other job, both these types of employees may slack off, for obvious reasons.

Ideally, the employees will work well *in spite of us*, whether we're there or not. We need to check ourselves and our employees and decide whether or not they work differently when we're present than when we're absent. This will tell us a lot about our style of motivation. If there is a difference, the motivation is external. If there's no difference, the motivation is internal. If this is the case, then it means that something about the job is motivating them internally to do the job well. This doesn't mean that they don't like or don't respect us; it doesn't say anything about their feelings toward us at all. They may appreciate us for leaving them alone. They may be irritated because we bother them too much. They may not even give us much thought. If they're doing their job, *then that's great*! We ought to get our ego satisfaction not from being liked or being respected, but from being good supervisors and getting the job done so well with the employees we have. Here's a little test to show how well our employees are motivated to work on their own, and whether or not we really believe they are. When we're away at a staff meeting or on vacation or in a training program off the job site, how many times do we call in to see if everything is going all right? This is one of the best measures of whether we think the job is getting done through internal motivation or not. Remember, if we have to be there, we still haven't reached the best style of supervision, especially as far as motivation is concerned. Let's see what we can do to see that employees do work more on their own.

WHAT SATISFIES PEOPLE?

For a long time we thought that people were satisfied, hence motivated, when we corrected the things that dissatisfied them. If they were unhappy with the temperature and we then corrected the temperature, we expected peak performance. If they were unhappy with the hospitalization program the organization offered, when we improved the program we expected work to increase proportionally. If they were unhappy with working conditions generally, or didn't like the parking facilities, or weren't pleased with the vacation policies, we thought that all it would take to motivate them to work harder would be to correct all these things. But those who have been around for awhile as supervisors know that when all these things were corrected (if they were indeed bad), we still didn't see much improvement in employee motivation. Some supervisors then decided that there was just no way to motivate today's workers (or make them happy). This was a dangerous conclusion, although it still exists in every organization among certain supervisors. It's particularly bad if some of the older supervisors manage to instill this philosophy in some of the newer supervisors, for if we don't understand what's happening, it's very easy to look at people's actions and draw this conclusion.

One way we can understand what really happens is to look at our own motivation. What is it that motivates us? What is it that makes us work harder? Is it the last raise we got? Probably not. Is it the great hospitalization program we have? Or the number of weeks vacation now granted by the organization? Not really. These aren't the things we look back on and use to explain why we really like certain jobs. Looking back at jobs we really were enthused about, we find that often they weren't the ones that offered the most money or the most benefits. We find that we aren't all that motivated by parking locations, vacations, and retirement plans, and even the last raise we got probably isn't causing us to work much harder or be more motivated. We may well complain when these "bad" things exist, of course, and they may even affect our work, but when they are corrected we aren't suddenly motivated to rush to the job every morning. In fact, if we weren't motivated before we got these things we most likely won't be *after* we get them. The truth is, these are still external motivators, because we don't really control them. When they are corrected, they don't change our activities, just the place where the activity takes place. The job itself is still the same.

WHY DO WE WORK HARDER?

If vacations, retirement plans, and other such benefits don't motivate us, what does? Maybe money? Well, we've already seen that the last raise didn't do much to motivate us. At least we aren't working all that hard just because we got it. After all, we *deserved* it—we had worked for it before we got it, so why put out harder now? Of course, if we had thought we deserved it and *didn't get it*, we would have been pretty upset. Our work would have suffered, no doubt. But getting it just brought us back to zero, so to speak. Now we may work harder in anticipation of another raise, so we can't rule out money altogether. But there has to be something else that will motivate people, because many of us have no control over the money our employees get—either they're on a schedule or under a contract or someone else has to approve their raises. So we can't use money alone as our motivator. In any event, we're still talking about an external motivator in a way. And what we do know is that the things that motivate people the most are those things that have to do with the job itself, rather than those things that surround the job. Let's look at some examples.

First, there is the matter of being recognized for the job we do. We like to have it known by others that we've done a good job or accomplished a meaningful task. No one has to put banners on the front of the building or across the parking lot. We don't have to see our name in lights, or in headlines in the organization's newsletter. The recognition can be as simple as a "well done" expressed in front of the boss or our co-workers. It can be a picture in the organization's newsletter or a mention of our name for some accomplishment. It can be getting to sign a job with our name, telling all who see it that we did the work or the planning or the figuring or the scheduling. It's a matter of gaining the status or recognition we mentioned in the previous chapter. We should note that this is a very powerful motivator, but it doesn't last very long. We are very excited for awhile, we show everybody our picture or our name, we listen to the folks congratulate us at lunchtime, and then it wears away. We may need some more recognition tomorrow or next week or next month, depending how much we got and how much we needed to motivate us.

"A little recognition on your part might have prevented this, J.B."

Another thing that motivates people is the chance to achieve and to know that the achievement has been made. This is especially effective if others know it too. It's a matter of seeing something all the way through and then being able to step back (literally or figuratively) and see a job well done. We like to see our work, especially if we've had the say-so all along and have received recognition for the work. A chance to achieve is more than just getting to look at the finished work, though. The fact that the organization thinks enough of us to let us do this on our own, *even if it's a simple task*, means a great deal to us and will motivate us as much as recognition. It is, of course, a form of recognition.

Responsibility is perhaps the most enduring form of motivation there is. Letting people know that the job is theirs, to do whatever they want to with it, *within the framework of the job requirements*, has a very lasting effect on the attitude of the worker. There are some requirements for giving responsibility, as we'll see, but this is an extremely potent form of getting people committed to do the work. The reason is pretty obvious; *commitment* is the key word. We all are simply more committed to things where we have the major responsibility for seeing the job through. Maybe the word "major" is the wrong choice, since it implies perhaps more responsibility than we're ready to give up to our people. It isn't intended that way. Even if we're talking about sweeping around the work area, the "major" responsibility would be in making the decision when to do the sweeping and when a satisfactory job had been done. It doesn't matter how big the job is, as much as how much of the job is really left up to the individual.

We said there were some requirements or rules for giving responsibility. Let's see what they are. First, there must be a willingness on the part of the receiver to take the responsibility. We shouldn't try to force employees to take responsibilities they don't want or are afraid of. Responsibility can be an awesome thing to some people. It may just be a bother to others. Some may see it only as extra work. Others may not be able to take the responsibility, even though they want to badly. We have to make wise use of this motivator, in other words. If we really intend to give people responsibility, we have to realize that we must also give them the right to make mistakes as well as to be right. Listen to this conversation between a boss, Karen Wells, and a subordinate, Dave Bradford:

"Now Dave, you've done a great job all along on this kind of thing, so I'd like to see you grow some more by taking some more of the responsibility."

"Why thank you, Karen. I have tried to put myself into the job as much as possible. It's nice to be recognized for a good job."

"Well, here's what I want you to do. From now on, you take the responsibility for answering letters that have to do with prepayments. I want you to write them yourself, and sign them, too."

"That's great! I've been doing rough drafts now for a few months, and I think I'd like to just do the whole thing myself."

"That's the reason I'm giving this to you, Dave. I've been watching the drafts and I have yet to find one that couldn't have gone out without my seeing it. Just remember, these are serious letters and much damage could be done to our image if they go out wrong."

"I certainly realize that, Karen. I've seen how much the clients worry about our answer and I've talked to a few on the phone. I'll be careful."

"I know you well enough to know you'll do just that. Remember, now, this is *your* job now. It'll be your responsibility from beginning to end. You decide what should be done, how we should put it in the letter, and then go ahead and write and sign the letter. . . . Er, there's just one thing I'd like to ask you to do for me, Dave."

"Yes, Karen, What's that?"

"Before you send anything out, just drop it by my desk for me to take a quick glance at it. . . . "

So what happened to the responsibility? Did Karen really give Dave the *responsibility* from beginning to end, or did she just give him the work to do from beginning to end? Actually, Dave left with no more responsibility than he'd always had. Up until now, he's been deciding what should be done, preparing a rough draft that never was changed, and Karen's been putting her signature on it. She was looking at it, giving the final okay, then letting it go out. What's going to be different now? Just that it's going to have Dave's signature on it, which may be some prestige, but certainly doesn't represent any new responsibility. What has happened is that Dave's now got the right to be right—which he always had—but not the right to be wrong. What will happen if the boss, Karen in this case, sees something she doesn't like? Obviously she's going to see that it's changed. If Dave does the job right, she'll let it go. If he's wrong, she'll catch it, and he'll change it to suit her. *Dave's still writing for her, not himself.* So how much commitment have we built into this "giving of responsibility"? Not much. If it really was all Dave's, he would have much more commitment. He'd work as hard as possible. If he had a question, he'd ask Karen about it. Now, if he's pretty sure, but not completely, there's always the chance that he'll put what he thinks is almost right, knowing that Karen will catch it if it's wrong. That's the difference in commitment levels. This is what we mean by giving the right to be wrong. It isn't easy to give; we have to be careful, and we have to be sure the employee can handle the job pretty well. Furthermore, we have to be willing to live with the possibility of mistakes, knowing that we may still have to bear the brunt of the error if it is made, since we aren't going to get into the "blaming business."

There is one last thing that motivates people to work harder, and this is the job itself. We can remember the jobs we had that were challenging, or meaningful, or served some good, or made us feel good because we were talented enough to do them. A job that is seen by the employee as being meaningful, whether challenging or not, can be very motivating. In today's world of work, it's often difficult to find jobs that *in themselves* are really all that meaningful. We've broken the jobs down into such small and insignificant parts that employees find many of them pretty dull and seemingly useless. Supervisors who have been able to modify the jobs slightly find that they can actually put some meaning back into the jobs. Sometimes it means pulling some of the activity of the next person in line back into this job, or adding more responsibility, or giving some of the meaningless work to a lower-level, less-skilled worker. The idea is to see that the employees realize that they are doing something that is meaningful to the total organization. It may mean great communications. It may mean letting the employees in on some of the decisions. It may mean that we go to them and ask how they can better organize their jobs into more complete units. Where this has been done, the results have been outstanding. Not only do the workers like the idea of being important enough to be brought into the decision-making process, but they've had some very good ideas as well.

ANTICIPATION PROVIDES THE MOTIVATION

Perhaps because of the way we word our discussions about motivation, we may sometimes miss the fact that we aren't motivated by a need for something. The motivation is in the anticipation of getting something to meet that need. If people need recognition or reward, they don't usually go around working very hard because they aren't getting any recognition or reward! The need exists because there is the absence of these things; the work comes about because there is the anticipation that if they do something well they'll get the recognition. There must be some reason to believe that the work will get the needs met, or else there won't be any motivation. It hurts us when people get needs met long enough (enough recognition, or feeling of belonging, or challenge, etc.) that they may lose their need. Hence the same thing that gave them motivation in the past may not work now. That's what's wrong with statements like, "Recognition is a good motivator," or, "Just let old ____ know that we need 'em and you'll see plenty of motivation." The things that motivate people may change from one time to another because of needs getting met or needs no longer getting met. As long as we understand that there has to be both a need and some kind of expectation that something the person does will help fulfill that need, we're less likely to be surprised when we do something that has always worked before and find it doesn't work anymore.

How does this work? We try to relate the task we're assigning the person to a need we think that person has. If the person seems ready for a challenge, hasn't had too many lately, and seems excited when we talk about a difficult problem we're not too sure about solving, it is a pretty good indication that there is both the need and the anticipation of fulfilling that need. As we make the assignment, we talk about the challenging aspects of the job rather than play it down. On the other hand, if we have an employee who has asked us several times how he or she is doing, or how he or she did on a certain project, we are seeing somebody who probably needs some recognition. Giving the same assignment to this person, and talking only about the challenge and not the reward, would be less likely to motivate the person. In fact, the sound of challenge may sound like a threat ("If I can't do it, I may be punished"). What will sound good to this employee will be words like, "Whoever gets this done will make a real mark for himself or herself," or, "If you can accomplish this, there's going to be plenty of excitement around here," or, "Not many people could be trusted with this. Since it's so important, I thought you were the one to give it to." Of course, it goes without saying that these ought to be true statements. Otherwise, we're just snowing them under and pretty soon it will come back to haunt us.

DELEGATING—FOR MANY REASONS

One of the problems with motivating people is that the best way to do it usually requires some delegation on our part. With delegation comes *risk* on our part. It is a difficult skill to learn, and many times—as we have supervised longer—we tend just to do the things ourselves rather than bother with delegating them. After all, we can do them quicker and better. If we expect to succeed as supervisors, especially to the point that we are not only doing our job well, but are also developing our people, we're going to have to delegate. There are many reasons why we delegate, most of them legitimate ones. Let's look at several and get some ideas about where delegation can best pay off for us.

Develop People

The most obvious, and perhaps the most popular, reason for delegating things to people is for their development. Since delegation means letting somebody do something that usually isn't his or hers to do, it is a good opportunity for employees to learn a new part of the work. We have to remember though, that just letting somebody do something they've never done before isn't going to cause them to grow *automatically*. As the saying goes, "Practice doesn't always make perfect, but it does usually make *permanent*." We may be just training people to do something wrong. If it's to be a learning experience, we'll have to make it such. We'll have to sit down with the people and go over their performance in doing the new assignment, showing them the right and wrong, the good and bad, and other ways of improving on the assignment.

Provide Time for Our Job

Sometimes, for no reason other than a selfish one, we need to delegate just to give ourselves a chance to catch up on our own work. Since there are so many good reasons why we delegate, there's nothing wrong with this, as far as the subordinates are concerned; and we can do a better job if we clear away some of the things that can be done by others.

Motivate People

As we've seen so often in this chapter, giving people additional responsibility is a good way to motivate them, if it's done under the right circumstances. One important aspect of responsibility is that much of it is in the mind. Having the responsibility for something is, as much as anything else, how the job or task is perceived. When somebody comes in and asks where to find something and the boss says, "Check with Mary, she's responsible for that," we've just added some responsibility to the job. Before we said that Mary was in charge of that part of the job, she perceived it as something we just told her to do; now she thinks of it as *hers*. This makes motivation easy, and it's something we can delegate without giving up anything.

Assess Potential

We'll never know just how well people can perform on a task that they have never done, no matter how much we've seen them do another job. If we really want to know how well somebody can perform, we give them that job to do—delegate it to them—and watch them. Of course, we have to be sure they understand that we *are* watching them. We need to let them know that we like what they've done in other areas, and want to give them additional tasks and responsibilities. We may even feel that some training is good for them before they start the job. In any case, we now have a means of assessing their potential in the actual job we're wondering about.

Recognition

Of all the needs we have, the need for recognition and status is probably the greatest. It therefore offers the best possibility for motivating people. There are some jobs which bring much recognition when they are delegated. Using the idea that responsibility is a matter of perception, we delegate in such a way that we give status and recognition. When we told Mary she was in charge of the task somebody needed help with, we gave her status. Remember that status requires two things to qualify:

- It must be something not many people have.
- It must be something that is perceived by others as valuable.

We have to be careful that when we delegate, we give real status and recognition and not just more work. If we had said, "From now on, Mary, I want you to help people do this job," we really have just said to her, "Now you have more work for the same amount of pay."

Show Requirements of Higher Level Job

People rarely know just what makes up a job which they haven't done before. If we let them do all or part of a task that is now being done by someone above them, we let them get a feel for it in a way they could never get in any other way. This is one way delegation pays off well. It may be that when the person tries out the new assignment, he or she may not like it, and hence will be happier if later on somebody else gets the job permanently.

Competition

When we delegate a job, we're saying that this is something we think that person can do. Implied, but not necessarily so, is the idea that *only* that person can do it right now. We don't have to make a big issue out of it, but we can use this often as a way to generate some friendly competition. When we delegate a job, and someone else comes around and wants to know why it wasn't given to him or her, we know several things. First, there was some status to the job because not everybody has it; and second, somebody thought it was valuable enough to ask about getting. We also know that we have generated some competition, and that there is some way that this assignment can be used in the future to motivate at least one other worker.

There are other reasons why we delegate, but the following will show us that there is also much merit in good delegation.

WHAT DO WE DELEGATE?

We could start better by asking, "What is it we don't delegate?" There are some things we should never delegate, no matter how busy we are or how competent the employees under us. For example, we should never delegate things that have to do with work rules. If we are making a *change* or a variation from the *standard work rules*, no matter how good our reasons, we should be the ones to tell people about it. Next, we should never delegate the *disciplinary aspects* of our job. If an employee needs some kind of reprimand for breaking rules or doing substandard work, we must do it instead of pushing it off on someone else. A third thing we should never delegate is the giving of *praise* or *recognition*. If employees have done something worthy of recognition, they're also worthy of receiving praise from us, not somebody under us. Finally, naturally we don't ever delegate anything that has to do with *policy setting*. Policy must come from higher up. If we are going to get respect for the policy, we should give it ourselves, not delegate it.

Now, recognizing that there is a great temptation just to delegate those things that we don't like to do or that become tedious to us, let's see some things we *should* delegate. We rationalize that even though these things are boring to us, they're a good learning experience for the person to whom we delegate them. Not only should we not delegate something just because we don't like to do it, but we also want to make sure that we have things being done at the level in the organization where it is most economical. We don't want to be responsible for having things done at a higher level—hence higher cost—than it's worth to the organization.

Rule Number One: *Delegate any routine or inconsequential matters.* It's not a matter of being nice and keeping some of the routine work away from people; it's a matter of getting things done at the lowest level where there is competence to do that job. Supervisors play an important part in the running of the business. Primarily they are paid to be thinkers, problem solvers and decision makers, not doers. We don't need to be embarrassed or shy about giving work we think is "beneath our job" to someone else. It probably is beneath us!

Rule Number Two: *Delegate things others can handle as well or better than we can.* Whether we like it or not, there are people under us who are just as competent and able to successfully perform a task as well as we are—maybe even more able. Most often it's something we did before we were a supervisor, and we are just hanging on to it. There may even be a little ego involved in all of this, or, as we discussed earlier, at least some feeling of comfort at being able to do something to completion and see the results (that's something we don't often get to do as supervisors). If somebody else can do it better and we have the authority to delegate it, we should always give serious consideration to delegating it to that individual.

Finally, Rule Number Three: *Delegate those things that will lead to the development of our subordinates.* We've already talked about this aspect of delegating, but let's note too, that when we're trying to delegate in order to develop subordinates, we ought to think of delegating a complete task, not just a part of the job. If there are deadlines to be met, they should have the responsibility for that, too. If there is some planning, let them do as much as possible. If there is contact with other employees, or even the customers or clients, let them in on that part. If there are some choices to be made, and they have the competence to make the choices, let them do so. If we do all the planning, make all the choices, contact all the people and meet all the deadlines, all they do is the work! They don't learn anything; they just got to do some work without any responsibility, reward, recognition, motivation, or satisfaction. Probably there was very little development.

CONCLUSION

How can we motivate our workers? We've seen several ways, both internal and external. We've seen that the things that motivate us the most are not those things that surround the job, although these are the things we hear the most complaints about. What motivates people is recognition, a chance to achieve, responsibility, and the job itself. If we expect our workers to perform just as well when we're not there as when we are there, we'll have to pick one of these things to get them motivated. We have to be careful, though, because it takes skill to know when and how to give these things to employees. We have to be serious about it. We have to mean it. If we want to know what motivates people, the best source to go to is ourselves and the jobs that motivated us!

DISCUSSION ACTIVITIES

1. Distinguish between external motivation and internal motivation, and give examples of each.

2. Discuss the reasons why just correcting things that cause people to complain (like parking spaces, poor insurance programs, less than desirable working conditions) often doesn't motivate people to work any harder.

3. List the ways in which responsibility can actually be harmful rather than motivational when given incorrectly.

4. Under what conditions should responsibility be given in order to get the most motivational value from it?

5. Discuss (debate) this statement: "It isn't true delegation if we reserve the right to pass on the assignment before it goes out."

6. Pick a simple job and find ways of building in job-enrichment factors.

chapter 7
TEAM BUILDING

All supervisors, both experienced and inexperienced, dream of that organization where everything runs smoothly. They see a place where there is no conflict among subordinates; where there are problems, of course, but where solutions come as a result of everybody working together as a team. They see an organization where everybody is watching everybody else, but not to catch them doing something wrong, or to find someone to blame for a foul-up of some kind, but rather to see where they might help out. They see a place where each employee sees the *real* assignment as the total job, not just a part that each individual contributes but a total of what everyone contributes. They see a place where people pitch in and help if there is a breakdown, even if the breakdown is not in their specific area. Communication is easy in this dream organization, because everyone *wants* to know what others are saying. Information moves easily up and down the organization as well as laterally. People are told what they need to know when they need to know it, and no secrets are reserved for a select group of managers so they can walk around with smug looks on their faces. People don't play games to get information or decisions. There are no under-the-table dealings, or politics, or promises of "you scratch my back and I'll scratch yours." There are still bosses and subordinates; there are still levels; there are still appraisals and even discipline if needed, but it rarely is. As we said, most supervisors dream of such a place or organization, but few expect to ever be working there—not in this life, anyway. Is there such a place? Do such organizations exist? What are my chances of supervising in such an organization? Well, such organizations do exist, and we can work in them. As a matter of fact, such organizations are *made*— they don't just happen. They can be made by any of us. It isn't easy, but it can be and is done. Such organizations come into being by a process we'll talk about in this chapter, a process called "team building."

THE HEALTH OF AN ORGANIZATION

Organizations, like people, can be healthy or unhealthy. Also like people, they have symptoms that tell us important things about their health. In a very real way, we can feel the pulse of the work group, or the entire organization, just by looking at certain things. Let's see what some of them are.

Attitudes

We've already pointed out that talking about attitudes is dangerous unless we have some specific standards to look for. In this case, though, we're talking about *general* feelings, about the organization, the other workers, and even about ourselves.

First, there is the matter of attitudes or feelings about the organization, the question of whether people see themselves as a part of the organization, or just outsiders employed to work there. This attitude deals with the question of how people view their relationship with their peers, subordinates, top management—all the people who make up the thing called an "organization." The organization becomes something of a personality within itself when all these people begin to do their jobs. The object of the organization, the service or product it handles, the budget, the expenses, the policies and procedures, all make up what we call an organization. Each person within that organization has some particular feeling about the organization. Usually, the feelings are similar.

Then there are the attitudes or feelings about the work. This is again an individual thing, but the general feeling that runs through the entire work group is the pulse we look for. How do people feel about their work or the jobs they do? How do they feel about the significance of their individual jobs as they fit with the other people's jobs? How do they feel about quotas? How do they feel about deadlines and completion dates? How do they feel about quality or service or keeping customers or clients happy and coming back? These are the symptoms we look for, and the pulse we feel when we want to check attitudes toward the job.

Finally, we look at the attitudes of the workers toward themselves. How do they feel about their own abilities? Do they desire to do better work? Do they feel that their own performance significantly affects the organization? Are they trying to meet their own personal needs on the job or outside of the work place? Do they see themselves retiring from this organization? Do they speak well of their own job, as though they are proud of it? Within these attitudes—toward the organization, the job, and themselves—lies the barometer to tell us how healthy the organization is.

Communications

Another area we look at in measuring the health of an organization is the all-important but often neglected area of communication. There is a hazard in talking about communication separately from the activities in the organization, because people often fail to relate the two. There are still those who don't recognize that communication is the tool by which we get information, give information, give out work, establish what work has been done, measure the quality of work, solve problems, make decisions, and generally carry on the business from day to day. Because communication is so important, it is a good basis for assessing the relative health of the organization. We will look at three different areas of communication.

First there is vertical communication, up and down the line in the organization. Here we're talking about multilevel communication—in other words, communication across more than one boss-subordinate level. We're talking about communication up and down the ladder from top to bottom. We're talking about not only what is said, how it is said, and when it is said, but also *how it is received.* Does one level pass on information as a matter of policy, while the next withholds information, saying that too much communicating causes confusion? Who is blamed for unpleasant communications? Are threats of any kind used? How much weight does something the "big boss" says carry, as compared to something one of the workers says that needs to be transmitted up the line?

Then there is the matter of communications between peers—not only coworkers, but interdepartmental peers as well. Lateral communication is important in that it tells us how well things are going as far as the organization's coordination is concerned. We can't effectively coordinate work with people we aren't communicating with. (Of course, communication failure between departments may mean that there is a healthy part of the organization trying to communicate with a sick part. We will have to look at both parts of the organization to tell for sure.)

Finally, we have to look at communications between the boss and subordinates. Ultimately, this is where the communications link is most often broken, and where some of the most serious damage is done when it does break. Perhaps one reason for the more frequent breakdowns in this area is that this is where the most communicating is done—all day, every day. So we look here for symptoms of sickness, for the true pulse of the organization. Even if a near fatal disease is striking at the overall organization, the organization will probably survive if this vital link stays healthy. We ask ourselves, is there constant communication on important things? Do we communicate too much? Not enough? Are the communication efforts successful? Are they ever painful? Are they on the level? These are the kinds of things we look at to see if the boss-subordinate relationships are healthy.

NEGOTIATING AN AGREEMENT

An important aspect of team building is to be able to get agreement between two people who may have some differences in their opinions, needs, or just plain likes and dislikes. There's nothing wrong with people having differences; the problem comes when this in some way leads to hostility or a breach in relations. Not only do the individuals suffer when this happens, but the organization does too. Sometimes the differences get so out of proportion that whole departments declare "war" on each other. No one will help anybody else, and people will even try to sabatoge each others' operations. That's sad, but it happens more often than we would like to think. How can we avoid this when the only problem is simply a difference between individuals? There are some good rules to follow. Let's see what they are.

The first key word is *"Confrontation."* We don't like confrontation, but sooner or later we will have to talk about the problem between ourselves and other people. There has to be a confrontation, but it doesn't have to be a battle. It doesn't have to be a shouting match. In fact, if it is either of these, it's not being done well at all. It needn't be that way at all. Ideally, it's just a matter of bringing things out in the open and talking about them. It can be initiated by either party in the disagreement, maybe with no more than, "Hey, I don't feel very comfortable with our disagreement over this. Can we talk about it?" Once we've cleared the air, we just sit down and get into the problem. Our job is not to prove who's right and who's wrong. Neither is it a matter of seeing that we completely have our own way. The primary goal is to get the matter resolved with each party getting as much satisfaction from the results as possible. That leads us to the second key word.

The second key word is *"Negotiation."* The very fact that there is a disagreement means that before agreement is reached we will have to do some negotiation. There are good and bad negotiations. The good ones are those in which each party has a chance to express opinions, feels the other person is listening, and believes the other person is being honest about the subject being discussed. Contrary to some of the things we hear about negotiating, this isn't a time to play games. It's a time in which trust must be high, truth must be told, and as much as possible, everything should be out in the open. If we feel uncomfortable, we say so; if we feel something isn't being dealt with, we bring it out; if we are disappointed in the way things are going, we admit it. The best thing we can do is to be open and honest; the worst thing we can do is to use something one party has said against another party. The first time we try to use some kind of trick to win a point, we've destroyed the trust and confidence, and the other person isn't about to be open again. The best test of our success is if we can come away from the negotiation better friends than when we came to it.

The last key word in negotiating an agreement is *"Compromise."* Again, there's something that doesn't sound right about the word "compromise." It sounds like we're not being as strong with our convictions as we ought to be. But that's not right. If each party is going to go away feeling good about the meeting, each must give a little. The idea is that in order to get something from the negotiation, we have to give up something. Before the meeting or confrontation we ask ourselves, "What do I really have to get out of this, and what can I possibly give up?" I don't purposely give away anything, but I certainly can offer something as a substitute if the other party isn't willing to take what is first offered (or if I'm not willing to give up what the other party wants). By the way, there is no need for the offerings to be equal. The value is not what we put on the thing given or gotten; it's what the other person puts on it. So, we've got the three rules for negotiating an agreement successfully. Disagreement is healthy; it says that not everyone is in the same rut. But it can become unhealthy if we let it cause a breach between the parties involved. If enough trust and maturity is shown, the parties will come away feeling good about the agreement, and very good about the other party. That's a pretty good solution all around!

Job Assignments

A final area we look at is that of job assignments. Is there an effort to provide for growth and development or are people placed in jobs by some whim of an obscure manager up the line? Here again we look at three different aspects. First, we must look at the opportunity for advancement. We have to find out if, under normal circumstances, there is a chance for people to move up in the organization. We need to know the promotion policy and if this policy is actually followed. We have to find out the relationship between skill and promotion to jobs requiring that skill. Further, we need to find out whether the appraisal system is used to mine new talent and new opportunities, or to "nail 'em to the wall." We need to know how much say the employees have in their own job placement. We need to know the organization's reaction to employees who ask to be considered for a different job than the one they're presently in.

In addition to knowing the chances for advancement, we need to know the chances for growth within the jobs the employees now hold. Is the job dead-end, with no possibility for challenge or learning new things, or is there plenty of room for making suggestions on ways of improving the job scope? Is there opportunity for additional training, either on or off the job? Are courses dealing with things a person might be doing on the next job available, so the employee can grow into the next job while still in the present job? Do the appraisals tell what the strengths and weaknesses of the employees are, and also provide for "career ladder" guidance? Do the employees see where their present jobs are leading them, and do these jobs allow them to use their present talents and develop new skills for future use?

Finally, what are the chances of employees getting better at what they are now doing? This is a major source of information about the health of an organization, and we must examine several aspects of this indicator. First of all, we must look to see if there is any *desire* on the part of the employee to improve, then look to see if the organization has the same desire for improving the employee. Are the employees just putting in time, waiting out the next raise, the next promotion (both of which may come automatically, regardless of skill), or even retirement? How much of their concentration is on being better in the present job and how much is spent on politicking for the next job? Is there an idea of perfection on the present job or a preoccupation about the next one? To accurately assess the health of any organization, we have to be able to answer these questions.

All of the above are barometers, thermometers, symptoms, indicators—whatever we want to call them. When we want to know how healthy an organization is, these are the things that will give us the best information. By the way, when we talk about an "organization," we may mean no more than one small work group, or we may mean the entire work force of a large concern or agency or service organization. We won't have time nor space to go into all these in detail, so let's just look instead at the characteristics of, first, an unhealthy organization, and second, a healthy organization. The symptoms will tell us where to look.

THE UNHEALTHY ORGANIZATION

There are many *good* indicators that *bad* situations exist in an organization. What we say is that the organization is "sick," or has problems. We'll just go through and list many of these problems, with some comment where necessary.

One symptom that's easy to spot is the matter of *tightening of controls when the budget is reduced.* The first thing that happens is that the boss begins to watch expenditures more closely, to insist that expenditures of smaller amounts be checked at his or her level. Even though there are those at lower levels who have the authority to approve the amounts, "You'd better check that with me from now on," becomes the watchword. Once this approval level is raised, it seldom is lowered again, even when the austerity program is over. People are afraid to ask for more money, even when they feel that the expenditure would save money in the short run, or that it would make a quick profit. As the approval level rises, decisions become harder to come by because of the overworked, underinformed nature of the boss's job.

The next symptom of a problem in the organization is when *tradition takes precedent over all else.* It doesn't matter what the new idea looks like, or what it might save us or make us; if we haven't ever done it this way before, we aren't likely to do it this way now. New employees have to learn the hard way because they don't know the traditions. Learning is often quick and painful, though. The first time a new employee comes up with an idea, suggestion, or action that varies from tradition, some smirk, some frown, some leave to avoid the bloodshed, and others just shrug until the boss lowers the boom with a "That's *not* the way we do it around here!" The key word is status quo, with "Don't rock the boat" being the motto on the masthead.

Then there's the problem of conflict. A sure sign of ill health is when *the most typical characteristic of an organization is the conflict* that exists between the employees both within and among departments. People draw little circles around themselves and dare anyone to cross over the line. People seldom talk to each other except to fuss or fume or fight. Things are misunderstood, almost on purpose, so there can be a good fight. People urge each other to get into fights. "You're not going to let them get away with *that,* are you?" is the cry to get people into battle. And, as is always the case with the brave and the true, no challenge can go unanswered. "We've got them now!" becomes the goal of every self-respecting supervisor-warrior. "They've been asking for it," marks the beginning of battle, and when it's over, little work has been accomplished, but everyone is exhausted from the bantering, jousting, and conflict that has made up the day. Conflict is one of the more obvious symptoms, of course, and is easy to spot. Other symptoms aren't that easy to find because of their more subtle nature.

For example, one less obvious but equally deadly indicator of an unhealthy organization is *the failure of the people to take an interest in the total project* being worked on. The employees may get concerned about their own little world of work, even show interest in it, but there's little interest in the overall project—either its success or its failure. There's just a general, lethargic lack of interest. Usually it's a mental shrugging of the shoulders, with little expression of regard for where the project is heading or for what they can do to see that it heads in the right direction. In its most serious form, individuals have very little interest even in their own work, but even when they do, if they have none in the overall project, the project doesn't come out very well. And finally, when it does work out all right, there's little reinforcement among the work force because there was little concern in the first place. As we've said, the results are bad, but the casual observer may miss these kinds of symptoms because there is little activity or discussion, as is the case with conflict.

Another subtle problem arises when *new ideas are not encouraged.* When ideas of any kind are turned down often enough, they finally just quit coming. The well goes dry, and no one is really aware of it. Problems are solved in the same old way, usually by the same people. Appraisals may even include statements about the employees not providing fresh ideas, but this doesn't do any good because of the lack of reinforcement when the ideas do come forth. The first reaction by the supervisors to a new idea is to find reasons why it *won't* work, rather than to find ways to make it work. Statements like "We've tried that before," "The time really isn't right for that right now," "It sounds good to me, but I doubt if the people upstairs would go along," and "You just don't understand the problem, or you would see why we can't do that," all go together as expressions of the symptom that new ideas aren't being encouraged.

The next symptom is a first cousin of the last one: the fact that *those new ideas that do come along usually come from the same people.* This is also a deadly illness, because it means that the minds and/or resources of all the people aren't being used, so there is a terrible waste of talent and brainpower. How is it that this happens? Simply because certain people get the reputation for having the ideas, and no one else can break into the society. New employees are told they'll have to wait; older employees are told they're out of date. Those who have the inside track through politicking or gamesmanship manage to freeze out the rest of the people. As in the case of the discouraging of new ideas, those who would submit solutions in the form of ideas soon get the message that their contributions aren't appreciated or listened to, so they give the work to others and become like zombies in the organization. They may cry a lot when at appraisal time they are told that they must not be very interested in their jobs, seeing as how they never offer any good ideas as to how the job could be improved.

Another indicator of ill health in an organization is when *organizational policies get in the way.* Even when good ideas come out, implementing them becomes so cumbersome that it's hardly worth the effort. One sure way to assess health in this area is to see *how many forms exist,* and how long they've been used. Of course, there's more paperwork than just the filling out of forms: memos have to be sent, clearances have to be obtained, notices have to be posted, and duplicates and triplicates have to be filed. All these myriad paper-handling chores can weigh down an organization for no real reasons. Part of this symptom is that once a form or a paper procedure is introduced it rarely ever goes out of circulation. It may get revised because it is no longer functional, but even the revision is looked on with disdain.

The next symptom of an ill organization is that *employees*—at all levels—*end up getting their kicks outside the organization* rather than inside. All of us are looking for recognition and achievement and some kind of ego satisfaction. Ideally this should be gotten on the job. When this happens, we work harder, are more motivated, and find satisfaction right at the work place without having to go outside. When we don't get these things on the job, we often go somewhere else—like to the parent-teacher organizations, the youth athletic associations, or religious groups. For every satisfaction we get outside the organization, there's one less that gets filled on the job, resulting in a slackening of the motivation and commitment to doing a good job. This isn't to say that everyone who does work outside the organization is merely looking for personal satisfaction. It does suggest, however, that when we find a large number of employees whose needs aren't met on the job, we'll usually find a large number whose needs are being met through a hobby or some other outside activity that is not job related. Watching where the kicks come from is a great way to feel the pulse of the organization.

Next comes the matter of change. What happens when change is suggested? How fast does change come? *When change comes hard, slowly, and painfully,* we know we have a problem in the organization. This is not just a matter of getting suggestions or ideas as we discussed earlier. It's what happens even when an idea is presented and accepted, and is characterized by the painfully slow process that has to be gone through in order for the change to result in action in the organization. People resist the efforts to institute the change. They find reasons to "study the situation a little more." They ask questions designed to scuttle the efforts to introduce new ideas or procedures or policies. While this often looks like an effort to keep from rocking the boat (and may in fact be just that), it's often just a case of "why change what we're all accustomed to." The problem is that no one cares whether or not the organization will be benefited by the change. People just don't like the idea of the personal inconveniences of making changes. It's a self-centered sickness, but the organization is the one that suffers in the long run.

Another symptom of organizational illness is when *the organization is very paternalistic,* usually taking on the image of the parent or protector. In this case, security is more important than challenge or growth. The organization, through the supervisors, worries about morale above all things. There are frequent "charm schools" for supervisors, and they are urged to "understand the employees" in order to keep morale high. There is the mistaken notion that "happy workers are producing workers," and attempts are made to provide everyone with a feeling of one big happy family, *even when production is low.* Discipline is put at the bottom of the organization's priorities, not because it isn't needed, but because it's deemed unnecessary and distasteful. People who speak of "production" are even frowned upon as being antipeople in some way. Explanations of "afterall, that's why we're running this organization—to get production" meet with cold and unbelieving stares. Production is a bad word!

The organization also has problems when most *managers/supervisors avoid any decisions or actions that are likely to include some risk-taking.* When decisions are made (often very quickly and with much commitment), they are made on the basis of which alternative has the lowest risk factor. Good, sound solutions are turned down or not even considered if they appear to involve some risk for the person carrying out the decision. Having to sign one's name to a project (or a decision or a letter) brings about fear and avoidance of the decision rather than building commitment. If this situation exists, we know that risk-taking is threatening in this organization. We know that we've got an unhealthy situation.

Another unhealthy sign is when *most managers*—except at top level—*have a low commitment to the organization's goals.* Earlier we talked about low commitment to and interest in the total project. Here we're talking about the *total organizational goals*—our reason for existing as an organization in the first place. People in middle and lower levels of management see goals as threats from top management and obstacles to getting the job done. Each year objectives are handed down from the top and sourly accepted by lower levels as unnecessary evils. Objectives are viewed as top management's way of putting pressure on, keeping people from doing their jobs "with enough freedom to operate." Seldom is an objective seen as realistic, and seldom is an objective set with any kind of consultation from lower levels. Mostly, objectives for the following year are set by upping whatever was reached this year by some fixed but unexplained percentage.

This suggests another symptom of organizational poor health: the fact that *lower levels are rarely consulted* about much of anything concerning the operation of the organization, whether it be setting objectives or increasing efficiency. Opinions of those at lower levels in the organization aren't considered as being worth very much, while the opinions of those at higher levels are considered virtually infallible. If there is a need for lower management to get into any decision-making aspects, their inputs are obtained and then they are dismissed while the real decision making goes on. Rarely will the people who contributed from lower levels be thanked for their inputs, though they may be openly *challenged* at the time the opinions were gathered. Certainly there would be no effort to inform these contributors of the final decisions as a courtesy, nor would any explanations be given as to why the final decisions were made as they were. While top management might ask, expect, and challenge inputs from lower management (and even non-management), this wouldn't be a two-way street. Lower management wouldn't be expected to share any information from higher management, such information being privileged data, belonging only to those in power. In fact, part of the power top management wields comes from its access to information that is carefully guarded and begrudgingly shared.

One of the most telling signs of organizational illness comes from watching what happens when mistakes are made. If *people are best known by the mistakes they make,* then there is a real problem. When top management (or management at any level, for that matter) takes the position that "there's no room for mistakes in this organization" they are also taking the position that there's little room for much *initiative* in the organization. This isn't to say that mistakes are to be encouraged—far from it. Mistakes can be a learning process, though, and should be. There has to be a limit to how many mistakes can be tolerated, and to what magnitude. The most serious mistakes are those that are *repeated*. There is really no excuse for this to happen, and when a mistake comes around again, made by the same person in the same situation, then one of two things must be true. Either the employee is careless (or unsuited for the job) or the supervisor failed to properly use the first mistake as a training exercise. But we aren't talking about the careless or poorly qualified employee. We're talking about that employee who is capable of doing a good job, does it most of the time, but makes that occasional error that proves the person to be human. What happens then? Is the mistake remembered longer and more vividly than the good jobs done by the same employee? When appraisal time comes around, are the mistakes used as an excuse to postpone a raise? If mistakes of even the competent and productive employees are remembered, out of proportion to their nature, then we have a strong indicator of poor health.

Closely akin to this is another symptom dealing with mistakes. What is the first action when a mistake is discovered? The answer to this question is critical in measuring the state of the organization's health. If *the initial effort is to find who's at fault and to place the blame,* rather than to overcome the error, solve whatever problems are caused by the mistake, and get on to the next project, then we have a sick organization on our hands. The question to be asked by the supervisor is not, "Why did you do it?" but rather, "What can we do to correct it?"

Still in the family tree of mistakes is another symptom dealing with interdepartmental relationships. Instead of cooperating with the people in the other work groups, *people spend time straightening them out.* They try to find ways to put the blame on others for any problems that arise, and will never admit that something they did caused a problem (even if they know it's the case). People are measured on the basis of their ability to pin the blame for a foul-up on someone in another department or work group. Here again, people aren't as interested in getting the job done as in placing the blame on someone else. Only after they've cleared themselves of any obligation for the error committed can they go about the task of overcoming the problems and seeing how they can prevent them from recurring.

Still another indicator of problems in the organization appears when no one in the organization feels that "this is *my* job." Instead of dealing with problems, or at least reporting them to someone who can do something about them, people just talk about the problems at break, or over lunch, or in the carpool going home. If something is driving away customers, or making clients wait too long, or keeping the organization from providing the proper service, people just keep saying, "*They* ought to do something about this." What is causing the sickness is lack of commitment—the same thing we talked about when we were discussing efforts to set goals and meet them.

Speaking of commitment, we also have a problem when *there is no commitment to doing things according to policy* or established procedure unless people feel like it. If people agree with the manual, then they'll follow it. If they don't, then they tell people to forget about doing it the approved way. Statements such as "We don't do it that way down here" are reason enough for people to violate the organization's established policies. There is no commitment to an organizational standard, and even when there is money spent to train people to work by the standard, the supervisors back on the job ridicule the training and tell the employees to forget all that garbage they learned in that dumb school. Worse yet, these supervisors are not accountable for whether their people actually do things according to the standard set by the organization. This problem could probably be traced back to top management if we were attempting to set the blame, but our effort is to show signs of unhealthy organizations, and this is one of them.

Another sign is when *people at all levels play games* with each other. No one considers handling a problem openly, or getting a decision by leveling with those involved. Politics are so rampant that even the newer people quickly learn the office games of handling certain people—buttering up some, threatening some, avoiding some, and always laying the proper groundwork before coming out and talking about a problem. (Groundwork in this case means covering trails, securing favorable data, hiding incriminating data, and so on.) There are constant efforts to go *around* people who are in the way rather than dealing with them in a forthright manner; and to make it worse, going around gets the job done better in most cases. This is because the organization lacks the proper health to get the job done in a straightforward manner.

One simple way of measuring much of the health of the organization—and identifying many of the things we've talked about here—is to sit in on a staff meeting. If these are occasions where there is much *telling from the boss,* with some questions from the staff for clarification of their duties but no suggestions as to what might or might not be done in the future, then we've got the symptoms of an unhealthy organization. If it's considered improper to question an action prescribed by the boss, especially if it's handed down as a top-management decision, then the symptom is loud and clear. The idea of the boss asking questions like, "What do you people think?" or "Do any of you have a suggestion?" or "Is this the best way?" or "How realistic is this goal?" would be unheard of in an unhealthy organization, and even if these questions did come out, the employees would be so shocked with disbelief or fear that they wouldn't give much useful data in return.

Finally, one last indicator of poor health: the appraisal. If *appraisal times are dreaded, or handled poorly, or not taken very seriously by either the boss or subordinate,* then we've got a good symptom of a bad situation. In these types of situations, the appraisal does little to move the employee toward better performance. There is little usable feedback, and a frequent imbalance of praise and criticism. Either the employee goes away feeling beaten to death because the supervisor used the appraisal time as a time to unload, or the employee goes away feeling almost perfect because the supervisor couldn't or wouldn't give out constructive criticism. Telling the employee that he or she was operating below standard would be too embarrassing for both the boss and subordinate, so all negative statements are brushed over or pushed aside quickly. Since this doesn't lead to any growth or satisfactory development, we have another bad barometer reading on the organization's health.

THE HEALTHY ORGANIZATION

We're likely to get discouraged if we read the foregoing list for very long, thinking that there's not much hope. Almost every organization suffers from *some* of the symptoms we've mentioned. But most don't suffer from *all* the symptoms, or all the symptoms *all the time,* or all the symptoms to their *fullest* extent. We need to recognize that the patient can still survive, and that just because some of these indicators suggest poor health, it's not necessarily a terminal case. There is hope as long as some signs of good health exist. What we need to do now is look for some of the good signs.

First, we look at the matter of commitment. Are the people really committed to getting the work done, and not just to getting by? In a healthy organization, there is *much effort not only to getting the job done, but to getting it done early* so the boss can have as much time as possible to look it over, to check for possible changes before taking it upstairs, or to just become familiar with the details for a better presentation to the staff meeting. If the boss says it would be good to get the work finished by a certain date, the employees know this is a realistic date, not a padded one to get them to work harder. Instead of everyone padding the dates for completion, with everybody knowing it's all right to take a few extra days, this system works in reverse. Everybody gives realistic dates, then tries to get through early.

Another healthy sign is when the different *subgroups, departments, and peer groups work together to solve problems,* rather than against each other. If one group comes up with a problem, the other groups not only accept the explanation on face value, but also pitch in to help as much as possible. When they pitch in they know that when they get into problems themselves, there will be help forthcoming in return. Instead of drawing battle lines around their jobs, the employees pull down barriers, cross lines for discussion with others, look at the job as the most important thing to be done, and take whatever steps necessary to accomplish this. In fact, the idea of "getting along" isn't even thought of as having much meaning; it comes naturally in getting the job done. When there is a crisis, no one asks why the crisis came about or who's fault it is. They simply ask, "What can I do to help out?" The central theme of the work operation is to get the job done and all energies are aimed toward that.

In healthy organizations, there is also an *honest approach to problems,* rather than a lot of under-the-table efforts to try to hide information or even hide the problems themselves. When there is a problem and someone is asked to help out, nobody thinks

"Next time don't ask for the boss's opinion—unless you want your idea changed."

about getting angry or suspecting the other of passing the buck. Each assumes that the other knows the job to be done, wants the job to be done well, and is doing everything possible to get it done. There's no effort to see if the jobs lie within the job description, because people recognize that this would have been checked already by the other person (although they would see the job descriptions not as restrictive measures but as guidelines).

Another healthy sign is when we see an organization *getting answers from people who have the answers.* This may not sound like much of a statement on the surface, but in many, many organizations the people who have answers and the people who have questions often rarely see each other. In healthy organizations, answers are respected on their merit, regardless of the level from which they came. Levels are respected as an organizational structure in the division of responsibility, but do not serve to separate the "good" ideas from the "bad."

To continue, *mistakes are recognized for what they are* in healthy organizations: the results of people working. Since few mistakes are made by people who do very little, in organizations enjoying good health there is an acceptance of a mistake as a means of learning. Mistakes certainly aren't encouraged, and there is frequent training aimed at preventing mistakes. The organization tries to prevent the mistakes with good controlling devices and frequent feedback usage. Even so, there is an understanding that people who are working will make mistakes and that those who make them are entitled to a chance to learn from them. Those who make the mistakes do not try to sweep them under the rug, but rather move quickly to undo any problems caused by the mistakes. The rule of thumb in such organizations is that a mistake can be tolerated, even expected on occasions, providing it occurs only once in the same situation. There is no excuse for making the same mistake twice, however; in this type of environment, this would generally be surprising and unacceptable.

Another sign of a healthy organization is that *most people enjoy their work.* It's not unusual to see people excited about projects, having an enjoyable time working on them. The job satisfaction comes from the work and the job, not from somewhere else like the bowling team or outside activity in community organizations. This doesn't mean that life is just one big party, with frequent visiting between desks and work locations just to pass the time of day. Time is respected for what it is: the means of accomplishing the tasks assigned. But there is an air of pleasantness about people in the group as they do their work. It is not just the spirit of cooperation, but goes deeper into the relationships among the workers, peers, and supervisors. The pleasant tone of voice used in the giving of an assignment; the willingness shown in accepting the assignment; the readiness to listen to a problem; the hesitancy to force an opinion on a subordinate; the willingness to listen to constructive criticism from above—all of these things indicate that this is a satisfying place to work. Job assignments are seen as opportunities to grow, not as unpleasant tasks. Workers are given opportunities to experience recognition in their work and to see and feel a sense of accomplishment in their activities. Motivation usually comes through having responsible assignments, but even the tedious tasks are approached as part of the job.

Still another sign of health is when *the energies of the organization are always funneled toward the job,* rather than toward procedures. Little time is spent in overcoming red tape, getting around people to get to the job, or waiting to get signatures, approvals, and answers. Policies that get in the way of getting the job done are modified or removed, not just accepted as "That's the way we do it around here." Policies are there, but they *facilitate* the work flow rather than get in the way. The old joke of "There's no reason, it's just company policy" has no meaning in this kind of organization. Decisions are easy to get, and whether the answer is yea or nay, at least the answer is given. There may or may not be an explanation for the answer, but the subordinates accept the answer as based on good judgment, not on vindictive treatment of the people involved.

Also a healthy sign is *mutual trust among the employees* at all levels. We've already seen how this works, but we should note that such trust is an excellent barometer of organizational health. When there is trust there is an accompanying openness that allows things to be discussed whenever and however they need to be discussed. Staff meetings, for example, aren't seen as battlefields, where people square off to get at each other or try to prove each other wrong in front of the boss. They're a place where problems are solved through open discussions, where pros and cons are put forth with no fear of punishment for "bad" thoughts. The trust level allows problems to be discussed from all angles; it allows people to say things that need to be said without a loud gasp running through the crowd, followed by a penetrating hush as everyone sits around uncomfortably waiting for the world to come to an end. This doesn't mean that conflicts don't arise, nor that feelings don't come to the surface on occasions. It does mean that such feelings are recognized as real and natural and can be dealt with in an adult way because everyone is dedicated to top performance. People expect differences of opinions and conflicts because they realize they will arise whenever people who are committed to getting a job done get together to solve problems about getting that job done. But these conflicts don't become a threat to survival. They are taken as a matter of course, and are solved between the factions involved in the normal course of events.

In healthy organizations, problems are solved on the basis of what's best for all concerned, and what will get the job done most effectively. Each person takes a portion of the responsibility for seeing that the job is done correctly and that the right decisions are made, even if this means that some people have to compromise their own likes and desires, or perhaps disagree with the boss on occasions. When the decisions are finally made, through negotiation or other means, they are respected and accepted as what must be done. Those who had to give up their "pet" ideas work as hard on the end product as those who had most of their ideas accepted. There is no gloating, no comments of "I told you so," no efforts to get even down the road somewhere—just a consolidated effort to get the job done as quickly and as well as possible.

IS IT REAL?

Is there such a world? Do people really work in places like this? Yes—such environments exist in places where there is a mutual understanding of the organization's goals and policies. Management doesn't just come around to the lower levels and say,

"Here's where you're going next year." Goals are discussed, increased, decreased, changed, and decided on after everyone involved has offered inputs. There is commitment because each person feels a part of the goals. The challenge is to get not where someone else has directed, but to where each person has helped set a target. It's a real world, all right. It's a world that can be created only with loving tender care by all levels of management. It can exist only when top management provides an umbrella for protecting it. It can survive only with constant vigil, with every level of supervision and management directing efforts toward it's survival. There is no conscious effort to practice a particular management style, but rather a flexibility in style to fit the people and the situations. And all the responsibility isn't on the management people. Even the hourly workers get caught up in the excitement of this existence. All of this doesn't happen overnight. It's a gradual, *purposeful* development, brought about by steps rather than by a sudden wave of the wand or by a written policy statement from the top of the organization. It cannot be ordered in, but will come about only in an orderly manner as the people in the organization get tired of the sick organization they've been working in.

CONCLUSION

As we said in the beginning, every employee—especially every supervisor—dreams of that organization where everything runs smoothly, where everybody is devoted to getting the job done without bickering and politicking. It is possible to have such a dream come true, but only when the organization reaches a healthy state of existence. We've seen the signs of poor health and of good health. The only way that the organization can have a clean bill of health is to develop a commitment to this dream and *start somewhere.* We've seen that the ideal is to start at the very top of the whole organization. If this doesn't happen, we don't have to sit back and bemoan the poor results and unhappy environment we're working in. We simply look at that organization *we're* the top of. What about our own health? This is the place to start. For us, and our limited sphere of influence, it's the only place we can start!

DISCUSSION ACTIVITIES

1. Discuss the role/responsibility of the supervisor in team building.

2. Why is it that some organizations develop a very healthy environment as far as team building is concerned, while others become very unhealthy?

3. Why is it that employees—even supervisors—frequently refer to a mystical "they" when referring to policy makers in the organization?

4. List as many symptoms as possible of an unhealthy organization.

5. List as many signs as possible of a healthy organization.

6. Discuss (debate) this statement: "No matter what the organization does, there will always be the need to place the blame when mistakes are made."

7. How does a healthy organization view and deal with mistakes?

8. What part does the level of trust play in the health of an organization, and how does trust come about?

chapter 8
CONSTRUCTIVE DISCIPLINE

The word *discipline* has a bad ring to it. There's just no way we can make it sound right. We can talk about "constructive" discipline, or "preventive" discipline, or "corrective" discipline, and it still comes out not sounding very good. Perhaps the reason goes back to our childhood days, when there was no way for discipline to be good whether it was done by our parents or our teachers. The idea of disciplining adults has an even worse sound to it. The fact is, as supervisors we have to discipline employees from time to time, because that's our responsibility—no one else can do it for us. We discipline people all the time, whether we realize it or not. Discipline is more (or less) than suspending an employee for three days without pay. It can be a casual reminder to an employee about taking the correct time out for lunch or break. It may consist of one word, a conference, a disciplinary interview, a warning, a suspension, or an outright dismissal from the organization.

Discipline is designed for one of two purposes: (1) to correct undesirable behavior, or (2) to prevent undesirable behavior from occurring in the future—behavior either of a particular offender, or of others who may be associated with the offender. Discipline takes place because somebody, somehow, has violated a rule or has failed to meet a particular, known standard of the organization. It may not be the most pleasant task, but it is necessary. Since it serves a very definite purpose, we should become skilled at it. Interestingly enough, those who have been supervising for a while will acknowledge that the better we are at discipline, the less we have to use it.

125

WHY DISCIPLINE?

We've already seen that we discipline because of irregular behavior of some kind. Such behavior is unacceptable and we cannot allow it to continue for several reasons. First of all, allowing one employee to perform below standard is bad for the morale of the other employees who work in the same group or who are in some way associated with this employee. When one employee is allowed to break the rules or not perform properly, the other employees resent having to meet the standard when one person doesn't have to. They not only resent that employee, but they will soon resent the supervisor and the organization and, if we aren't careful, will begin to perform less well. If we allow the behavior to continue uncorrected, the other employees become frustrated; they look to us to do the correcting and disciplining, and when we don't they see us as failing in our job.

Another reason we discipline is that when one employee is performing below standard and the rest of the group knows it, we have an unhealthy organization. There's very little chance that we'll ever get much of a team effort until the correction is made. There will be those who see the misconduct as interfering with their job (and they're probably right), so they see their job as being made harder by this person. They may feel that because this employee is allowed to continue below standard, they themselves are no longer able to get as much done in the same amount of time as before. Naturally, they're going to resent this extra load, as they see it. Even other work groups may be affected if we aren't careful. If they see one of our workers being allowed to get away with substandard behavior, they'll be quick to blame our group if the slightest thing goes wrong. Even if we're not at fault on the particular item or action in question, we really won't have a leg to stand on when it comes to trying to defend our position.

Finally, there's the matter of *effectiveness*, both our own as supervisors and the employees' as workers. We've seen that the other members of the work group will probably suffer as far as their effectiveness is concerned. And the worker's own usefulness and effectiveness will diminish considerably if the substandard behavior is allowed to continue unchecked. If the employee knows that the supervisor knows about the poor performance, or the breaking of the rules, and sees that the supervisor isn't going to do anything about it, there isn't much hope that the performance will improve of its own accord. At best the performance will continue at the same poor rate, and at worst it will decline even further. (Since sooner or later we'll have to deal with the employee, sooner is much better than later. Unfortunately, many of us treat the need for discipline like a stray dog: we just ignore it, hoping it will go away!

PROBLEMS WITH DISCIPLINE

Since it's obvious that we should discipline when necessary, why is it we don't have a good discipline program going all the time? Well, there are some problems with discipline, and it isn't as easy as we think. It's a skill that requires plenty of time, experience, and training. Let's look at some of the problems we're likely to run into if we begin disciplining where we haven't before. If we suddenly decide to take action in situations where we've formerly allowed a below-standard performance to exist, we'll find that the employees will wonder if we're really serious. They'll immediately see the inconsistency in our supervision, and this makes it hard for us to discipline properly. "How come you're starting to complain about this now when you've let it go without saying anything before?" is a difficult question to answer, and an even more difficult position to defend. *Perhaps nothing will haunt us more in the long run than inconsistent supervision.*

Another problem we'll run into is that when we postpone action, and then have to discipline, we'll probably be acting under stress—and that's almost always bad news. We may be acting now because the situation has gotten so bad that we can't allow it to continue any longer. This means that we're dealing with a big problem that should never have become that big, so things are now out of proportion to what they ought to be. We've got to get the sledge hammer out to do a job that a tack hammer would have done a little while ago. What's worse, we may have to take action because *our* boss is getting on us, which means that the problem has gotten out of hand and is now seen as serious at the next level up in the organization. Now we're acting out of panic. We have to rush in and do something about a problem because somebody above us has forced action from us.

We probably won't act in nearly as rational or objective a way as we should because of the pressure. What may be even worse is that in our panic we may try to blame our boss as a way of explaining our sudden spurt of action. In an effort to clear ourselves, we may commit an even graver error by not taking the responsibility for our action. It's easy to blame the boss, and it's effective *at the time*, but sooner or later we'll have to live with the fact that we've passed the blame up to someone else for something we are supposed to be responsible for.

We may discover that there are other sources of pressure, too. The pressure may come from our peers—the other supervisors we work with. It may be that they are unable to control their employees because we are letting one or more of ours get by with things that are unacceptable to our peers. Our cosupervisors get tired of trying to get their employees to perform to a certain standard, even disciplining them if they don't, only to find that right next to them are employees who don't have to meet the same standards. When we get that kind of pressure, we almost have to act. But it's too late because the motivation is wrong. This is also true when the pressure comes from the other employees who are trying to do their job but find the substandard employee interfering with them. If they come to us or in some other way demand that we take some action, we're under pressure to act, and must act, but for the wrong reasons again.

Another problem we have in disciplining arises when we don't have a good alternative action for the behavior we don't like in the employee. Just to tell the employee to "do better" isn't going to get very satisfactory results. If we call an employee in and say, "You've got a bad attitude," without defining the behavior that causes us to say that and without describing a behavior we'd prefer, then we're not doing a very good job of disciplining. We're in real trouble if we think we can get good behavior out of people just by criticizing the bad behavior. We may get them to stop doing the wrong things, but we aren't very likely to motivate them to do the right things. This goes back to the need for a standard. If we don't have a standard of performance that's clear to the employees, then we shouldn't begin to do much disciplining. Also, if we have no standard, we say strange things to our employees in the form of discipline. We say things like, "One of your problems is you complain too much." Now, we all know employees who complain, we get tired of it, and we think it interferes with the performance of the other employees. But we can't just tell an employee to stop complaining. After all, how much complaining do we do? Are we willing to give up our complaining? Do we have a bad attitude because we complain? "Wait," you say, "our complaining is all worthwhile complaining, and besides, we don't complain as much as our bad employees." Okay, let's grant that that's so, even though we're on shaky ground with that kind of reasoning. All we have to do now is tell the employee what the standard is for worthwhile and non-worthwhile complaining, how much complaining is enough, and how much is too much. (Six times a day is all right; seven or more is too much?)

Perhaps the worst kinds of problems will be created when we end up disciplining employees to *get at them.* For some reason we don't like an employee, or don't like the employee's attitude, and we end up feeling pretty vindictive toward this employee. We set our minds on wanting to get something on the employee, and sure enough, we get it. (What employee do we have who we couldn't get something on if we put our efforts to it?) The problem comes with our frame of mind as well as our purpose in disciplining. We're foolish to go into a disciplinary session with an employee when we've had to work this hard to find some reason to be in the session. Our chances of being objective are almost nil, and our ability to choose proper kinds of corrective action or appropriate penalties is going to suffer terribly. As we'll see later, the only hope we can have for discipline to work is for us to be unemotional about it, and if we're acting out of vindictiveness, then we aren't likely to be unemotional when we do get around to disciplining this employee.

One problem that often arises, though not as often with experienced supervisors, is when we really don't have the confidence we ought to have in ourselves as supervisors. Even though the organization chart says we're the boss, we feel for one reason or another that we don't quite have the clout to make discipline stick. We may even lack confidence in our skill at disciplining. If either of these is the case, then we're going to have some real problems when we start to do our disciplining. One thing that affects our feelings about having the authority to discipline is when we've failed to get the backing on previous occasions. It's quite easy to just say, "What's the use? Management won't back me up anyway," and then not do any disciplining. As easy as it is to feel that way, we still can't capitulate on the job because of all the reasons we mentioned earlier in this chapter. We have to do our job—all of our job—even if we suspect that the backing isn't going to be there. If the managers above us don't do their job, then that reflects on them. If we don't do our job—whatever the reason—it reflects on us.

WHY DON'T WE DISCIPLINE?

After all we've said about discipline and the reasons for it, why is it we don't do more of it? Why is it that many of us avoid it as though it represented the plague or something? Those who've been supervisors for quite some time and who have been engaged in discipline will have a ready answer to these questions. Let's see what the roadblocks are that keep us from doing the discipline we should be doing. We've already mentioned one reason, by the way—the matter of lack of confidence. Many times we just don't know where to start or what action to take or how to take it, so we don't do anything, compounding the problems as we've seen. But there are some other reasons for our not carrying out this responsibility in better fashion.

Perhaps the most obvious obstacle is that discipline is often unpleasant. As we said at the beginning of this chapter, even the *word* sounds unpleasant. It doesn't matter that we realize that we should do it and that everybody and everything may be better off if we do do it—because we think of it as being unpleasant, we don't do it. Much of the unpleasantness is in our own minds, of course, and we conjure up all sorts of terrible things that might happen if we discipline the person needing it. This is not to say that we haven't experienced some unpleasantness in the past with discipline. It does say that our experience is working against us rather than for us. We know we should do it, we know that the responsibility is there, but our past experience tells us that it's not going to be much fun. Our imagination and our experience get in the way of our doing what we should be doing. It's almost as though we'd be better off it we didn't have any experience at all. We might need to get hold of our imagination, too. We envision the employee getting angry, or quitting, or starting a revolt, or even shutting down the operation altogether. As bad as things sometimes get, they rarely ever get as bad as we imagine.

This leads us to another reason why we avoid discipline: our procrastination has gotten us into trouble. Because we have waited so long, let things slide along, allowed rules to be broken and employees to work below standard, all without taking any action, we may have gotten things into such a mess that there are going to be serious consequences. There's a basic rule of thumb about procrastination: *unsolved problems rarely get smaller or go away; they nearly always remain and get bigger.* This being true, if we fail to solve a small problem with discipline when it first comes up, we allow the problem to come to a boil and it takes all the skill we can muster to solve it in the end—and even then we will come out only by the skin of our teeth.

A final reason why we don't do the disciplining essential to good management is that somewhere earlier we've failed to establish the proper amount of openness in our communications. We just don't know how to talk to our employees very well. We can talk to them about sports, about television shows, about the weather, even about doing the job correctly, but we just can't communicate well enough with them about deficiencies in their performances. We need to be able to talk to our employees in an adult, rational way, but in our day-to-day activities we may have failed to establish the right kind of base that allows us to talk to the employee about things being done wrong as well as things being done well. If we're going to be successful in our rough moments, like when there is a need for plain talk and discipline, we're going to have to lay the foundation on the job every day with our regular communications efforts.

ALTERNATIVES TO DISCIPLINE #1

Suppose we don't do any disciplining—is there an alternative? Let's look at some. Suppose we don't do anything. That's cer-

"It all started sixteen years ago in the executive washroom—and the rest is history."

tainly an alternative. It may be the one we most often choose. We either procrastinate or just decide to ignore the problem altogether, hoping it will get better. We may get in a few snide remarks to the employee, may even joke without smiling very much, but nothing that could be called direct discipline. How does this really work? Experienced supervisors can tell us that things usually get worse, not better, and we've got to live with the frustrations of knowing that sooner or later we'll still have to do something. All the time our conscience may be bothering us because we know we should be doing something about the problem, especially if we see the problem every day. If we haven't done anything, then finally have to take some action, we'll find that the employee is going to be unhappy, the situation is going to be worse than it should have been, and we start the procrastination process all over again.

We've already mentioned another alternative to doing the disciplining: we can pass it on to someone else, usually the boss. We may even get our boss to come and talk to our people, hoping the guilty party will pay close attention. This may work, but it will be close to a miracle if it does, and besides, we've really abdicated when we do that. Who's going to take care of our next discipline case? Are we going to have to get the boss to do all our "hard jobs"? Another solution is to get the boss to use his or her name, and therefore take the blame. We try to stay on the good side of our employees by telling them the boss is unhappy with the way they are performing. The implication, of course, is that we're satisfied, but we'd better satisfy the boss. That makes the boss the heavy, and us the nice guy. The truth is, this is just another case where we've failed to take the responsibility that is ours, and we certainly haven't done the boss any favors, either.

THE OPTION OF TEAM BUILDING

One option we haven't talked about would mean much less discipline if we used it. This is to develop a work situation where *there is no need for discipline.* This should appeal to all of us, but where is this never-never land beyond the rainbow? This place where employees perform in such a way that no discipline is required—or at least very little? This place where employees exercise self-discipline, care about their jobs, and even help others with theirs if the going gets tough? This place where employees feel a responsibility toward their jobs, their coworkers, their organization, even us as their boss? The place we're talking about, of course, is where we have developed a *team effort*. Team effort is created through *team building*, which is essentially a process of sharing the responsibility with those below us to such an extent that they develop commitment to and accountability for the job. They do the work because *they* see the need to get it done, because *they've* had some inputs into the goals, and because *they've* been asked for their opinions on matters that concern them.

What all this amounts to is that we no longer have to *drive* people. They are allowed to make some of the decisions, feel a part of the job, feel that what they're doing is meaningful, and generally take a different viewpoint toward their job, because *we've* taken a different viewpoint toward their job. Now before we get too far into thinking that we've solved all our discipline problems, let's hasten to point out that when it's time to use discipline, it's too late to use team building. Basically, the use of discipline is the symptom of an unhealthy organization. If things are running smoothly, there shouldn't be a need for much discipline. The need for discipline arises because things have gotten fouled up (and not just with the workers, either) and we've got to step in and correct the situation. This doesn't mean that the workers aren't at fault, but they're not *always* at fault! Let's take a look at some reasons why people don't work and see if we can discover some of the things that we as supervisors fail to do that, if we did them, would provide us with some team-building exercise.

WHY DON'T PEOPLE PERFORM AS THEY SHOULD?

When we talk about discipline, we're talking about an action taken against an employee who has failed to perform properly, either by failing to do something that was required or by breaking some rule or policy. As we've said, when it gets this far it's too late to embark on some team-building program that will extend over several months. When the performance is below standard or there's been a violation, it's time to take disciplinary action. And it's also time to look at the employee and find why his or her performance wasn't up to what we wanted it to be. In other words, why don't employees perform as they should? Obviously, there are many and varied reasons, so let's look at some of them in detail.

Lack of Standards

Perhaps one of the most overlooked reasons why people don't meet the standard is that *there is no standard.* Take the case of the employee who leaves early. One supervisor may allow the employees to leave a little early to miss the traffic, providing their work is finished and satisfactory. What was the standard for this job? Suppose there was a real whiz who could complete the job two hours before quitting time? Would we allow this employee to leave early? If the answer is, "No, we can't have anybody leaving *that* early!" then we have to decide how early is "that" early. We can't just say that it's all right to leave early, but only a "little" early. Any time we've got a word or standard that's open to interpretation, we've got a weak standard. For example, if the next supervisor comes in and says "Nobody leaves before quitting time," then we've got a very precise standard— *providing the workers are informed.*

One of the basic rules of standards is that they must be known and understood by both workers and supervisors. It's too late to explain the rule or standard for the first time when we start to discipline an employee. The new supervisor coming into a situation where the previous boss had allowed for early departure might not know that this was the standard. When the employees begin leaving early, even if it isn't "that" early, then the supervisor sees a group of employees who seemingly need disciplining. The supervisor says, "I've got to stop all these employees from leaving early. They aren't taking any responsibility at all for their behavior. They're going to set a precedent!" Actually, the precedent has already been set. The newer supervisor is actually going to have to *break* a precedent, not prevent one from being set. So we've got a case where the supervisor didn't operate on the same standard as the employees, and the results were "below standard" performance.

Conflicting Standards

Another very distressing reason why employees don't meet certain standards is that there are *conflicting or opposing standards.* As we understand one standard to mean such and such a thing, and try to meet that one, we discover that there is another standard that will compete or even prevent this first one from being met. In other words, if we meet the first one, we'll not make the second and vice versa. For example, we tell a worker to work safely, always use an approved ladder, and not run. Then we get in a hurry to meet a production standard and realize it can't be met this afternoon unless we get certain adjustments made up above the line, so we shove a box over and tell the employee to get up on it and fix the problem—or to *hurry* down and get the ladder out of the store room. As a further example, we may tell a sales clerk to always try to move some of the poorer moving items whenever there's a sale to a customer. We also set a limit on how much time should be taken in selling something to a customer. When there's a crowd of people waiting, and we hear the sales clerk trying to move the slow-moving items, we may get upset and say that the clerk is taking too long for the sale. We have competing standards, in other words. We know what will happen, of course. The clerk or the assembly worker will give in to the pressure, doing that job that involves the most reward and least punishment and letting the other go.

Lack of Training

Another reason employees don't perform up to standard is that they may not have been trained for the job. There's no reason to think that employees will just crawl out from under a rock and be able to perform without any training at all, and yet we act as though we expect them to do just that. If we expect employees to perform properly we'll have to train them properly. There's a basic rule here, too. In fairness to the employees, they should be neither appraised nor disciplined until they've at least shown that they could once do the job. This means that they must not only *understand* what it is they're supposed to do, but also know *how* to do it and *be able* to do it. That's where training comes in. We won't go into training in much detail here, but let's at least point out that good training is more than just showing the employees how to do something, asking if they've got any questions, and, if not, assuming that they've been trained. The record may show the time has been spent, and we may call it training, but it certainly wasn't very *good* training.

Lack of Feedback

Employees also don't perform as we want them to because they don't get adequate day-to-day feedback on their work. They may get an appraisal once or twice a year but they really couldn't say for sure just how they're doing on any given day or at any given task. Those of us who've been around awhile know that the last month or so can have more influence on an annual appraisal than the rest of the whole year. (Even the last couple of weeks can have their effect if the employee suddenly starts to look very good, as we'll see in Chapter 9.) There should be no surprises at appraisal time. The employees should be well enough informed along the way that they know just where they stand. The important thing is that they know how they are doing, and receive frequent feedback, reinforcement on what they do well, and whatever correction is needed. This allows the job to flow in an orderly fashion, instead of fluctuating up and down as often happens when annual appraisals are the only form of feedback.

It's really not such a task to keep employees informed on their performance. The procedure requires that we keep the communication lines open, but also that we keep the communications on such a plane that we can correct as well as commend without having a major problem or conflict. If we have a problem when we inform an employee of substandard performance, then the problem is deeper than the performance; the problem is one of not being able to level with our employees, and that's serious. It will prevent any hope of team building, since team building is based almost entirely on the leveling process.

Incorrect Reinforcement

Incorrect reinforcement is a further reason for poor employee performance. Take the case of the assembly line worker. When the line is about to go down and the employee jumps up on a rickety box and fixes the problem, and we tell our boss *in front of the employee* how the thinking of the worker saved the line from being shut down, we've reinforced a *nonstandard* performance. We shouldn't be surprised later on when—on a routine assignment —the employee is found up on that same rickety box working. When we gather our sales clerks together for a review of sales and point out our star clerk who has sold more of the poorer sellers than anyone else, we can expect that an inordinate amount of time is going to be spent on trying to sell these items in the future.

We also find that we sometimes fail to reward good performance, which will often result in the work suffering over a period of time. Many supervisors we are familiar with take the position that employees are paid to perform correctly, hence don't need any rewards for just doing their jobs. This reasoning is probably all right, but the results don't support the theory. People tend to repeat those behaviors for which they receive some reward or recognition, and tend to let slip those things for which they are not rewarded. If we expect an employee to perform something well, we'll have to reinforce that behavior on occasions when we see it occur. Not every time, but often enough to let them know that we know and care about the good performance. This is more than just feedback—it is *reinforcement for doing the right thing.*

Bad Organizational Environment

A final reason we'll discuss as to why employees don't do their job is the fact that the whole atmosphere may be bad as far as organizational climate is concerned. There may be a lot of friction among the workers. They fuss and pick at each other. They set up artificial battle lines and dare each other to cross these lines. They form cliques and one group doesn't speak to the other. Information is guarded and nobody gives out any information voluntarily. Everything is played "close to the vest," as it were. There is a sharp line between the boss and the subordinates and there is open competition between them. Workers do no more than is absolutely necessary and the bosses drive and push for as much as possible. When a mistake occurs, the first action is to find someone to blame, not to solve the problems.

Altogether, that's a very unhealthy organization, and the need for discipline would normally be very high in such a working environment. We can be sure that very few people would be working up to standard unless they were forced to by their supervisors.

How does this happen and what can the supervisor do about it? When the situation gets as bad as the one we've just described (and experienced supervisors can testify that such situations do exist), there is no magic formula for curing it. The cure not only will require the proper action by everyone's supervisor, but will also take a long time, perhaps even years. Furthermore, it will take the skill of good, experienced supervisors working with much diligence to correct it. We can't sit back and expect it to get better all by itself. We can't expect the workers to change of their own accord. We can't wait for them to "straighten themselves out." The only way change will take place is for there to be a direct approach, with a specific plan, that is accepted and practiced by all levels of management. We won't go into the details here, since our discussion is on why employees don't always perform. From what we've said so far, though, it's easy to see that when an organization is as sick as the one we've mentioned, performance will most likely be substandard by many if not most workers.

Up until now we've talked about reasons for poor performance that aren't really the employees' fault. What this means is that we have to be careful if we attempt discipline in cases like this. We've talking about one of the inequities that plague supervisors, and one that is much more familiar to older supervisors. We have an employee who is performing below standard—maybe by breaking rules, maybe by insubordination, maybe in a serious way, maybe in a mild way, but nevertheless not performing as we desire. This cannot go unchecked. It may be influencing the other employees, as we've said. The violation may have a hard and fast, well-known penalty. We have to exercise discipline. Yet, in the face of all this, we still know that in large measure, we're responsible for the behavior that we're seeing. The performance of the individuals under us may have taken a long time in developing to the point we're now seeing, but if the conditions we've been talking about in this chapter exist, and we've allowed them to stay that way, then we're watching the results of our supervision, and having to discipline for it. As we've said, we don't have much choice, but it ought to cause us to work a little harder to see that other employees don't end up the same way!

CHARACTERISTICS OF GOOD DISCIPLINE

Why is it that some people can handle discipline and others have difficulty? The reason is that one has developed a skill the other hasn't. What, then, does good discipline look like? What are the characteristics of good discipline as opposed to bad? They are obvious for the most part, but let's review them.

Fairness

The first thing the experienced supervisor will say, speaking from *sad* experience sometimes, is that the first and most important characteristic of any discipline is that it be *fair* to all concerned. That's not hard to accept. Most everyone would agree that fairness is among the most important considerations in any dealings with people. The problems arise when we start trying to get a good, clear picture of *just what is fair?* We've just finished talking about a situation where we had to discipline employees for conduct that we may well have caused ourselves over the period of time we had supervised them. If we ask ourselves if that's fair, we'd be in trouble if we said yes (in trouble with our conscience, at least).

In discipline, fairness isn't so hard to define, however. It means that what we do *is the same thing we would do to anyone else under the same circumstances.* We don't let our likes and dislikes interfere with our actions. The fact that one of our favorite employees has violated a rule and we have to exercise discipline doesn't keep us from doing it. We don't play favorites. As we'll see later, we do take into consideration extenuating circumstances, but these should be based only on the actions of the employees, not on whether we like the employees or not. Being fair means that the discipline we choose matches the offense or violation committed. We don't try to teach people lessons when the offense doesn't warrant it. And we choose the same penalty for the same offense, unless there is a rule for repeated violations.

Absence of Emotion

The next characteristic is about as difficult to maintain as is fairness: the *absence of emotion*. It sounds easy enough; we just go about our discipline without regard to our own feelings. After all, the employee has violated a rule. The evidence is there, we've got justice on our side, so what's there to be emotional about? That sounds like a new supervisor who's been reading too many books. The fact is, that employee works for us and we're going to dispense some discipline that will probably affect the employee's life in some unpleasant way. There may be loss of pay, loss of prestige, and/or some loss of self-respect. Maybe the discipline shouldn't have these results, and it doesn't always have to, but it nevertheless may. And we have to see that employee every day. We have to get work out of that employee every day. We're responsible for the conduct of that person on the job for as long as he or she works for us. It's almost impossible for us to discipline without some feelings. Okay, so what do we do? One thing is that we don't discipline in such a way as to create a big scene. We do it in private, quietly, without raising our voice. If there is argument, we don't participate in an argumentative way. We answer questions, but we don't become defensive. We explain, but we don't "lord it over" the person. We maintain our role as supervisor, but we don't make a big issue out of who's the boss. Another way to avoid an emotional experience is to try never to discipline when we're angry. If we're having trouble calming down, we'd better look for something else to calm our nerves besides discipline. When we exercise discipline while we're angry, we may end up losing our judgment or not be as objective as we should be. We may not listen very well to the employee's side of things, and may find ourselves regretting this later on.

Sometimes we get emotional because we're disciplining for the wrong reasons. It may be that we've been wanting to get at an employee for a long time, and when we finally catch the person in a violation, we pounce like a lion. There's no room for vindictiveness in supervising people, so we can't go around trying to get at people. If we do, *we may miss some of the good things they're doing.* In the long run, we must think in terms of meeting first the organization's needs, then the employees' needs, and only then our own. When we discipline out of anger, we may be putting our own need first, ahead of everything else. Another problem with disciplining out of anger, or when we're angry, is that we will find it difficult to convince the employee that our goal is to get the job done properly, not get even with the employee. We'll find it hard to show that we're looking after the organization's interest and that's all we want to accomplish. Our emotions may get in the way of our words. Our actions and looks may overshadow our rationale.

Timeliness

While we don't want to discipline in anger, we do want to discipline at a time *as close to the violation as possible*. We want to do it while the action that caused the discipline is still fresh in the mind of the violator. We don't want to wait until the employee no longer remembers just what it was that was wrong; by this time the violation may not seem nearly as serious to the employee—nor to us, for that matter. In addition to forgetting what the discipline was all about, we may have the added consideration that the employee is now engaged in doing something very well, or at least satisfactorily. We find ourselves needing to discipline, but not wanting to discourage good behavior. All of this simply says that we should get the discipline and the violation as close together as possible.

Absence of Surprise

This leads to the next characteristic, which in some ways is part of the same one—the *circumstances surrounding the discipline should be understood by the employee*. There shouldn't be any surprises where discipline is concerned. The employees should understand *before* the violation what they can expect if they don't perform up to standard in some way. In most cases, the procedure is to explain the standards, make sure the employee can perform correctly and understands the policy about discipline, then give some kind of warning (usually recorded in the record) if an infraction occurs. Then when the violation happens again, the discipline should be a natural consequence. The employee understood the rules and the consequences of violating those rules, so there should be no quarrel with any of the proceedings. Let's be sure that we understand that when we go through these procedures —the explanations, the warnings, and the documentation—we aren't trying to catch the employee or gang up data to over- whelm the employee with our prowess at disciplining. What we want to make clear to the employees is that our aim is to *get the job done correctly*. This is critical, because when we're in the warn- ing stage, we can very easily make it sound like a threat. Even if we don't intend for it to sound that way, the employee may in- terpret it that way because of the timing. We just have to keep emphasizing that we're glad the employee is here, and that we know that the goal of both of us is to get the work done in a pleasant but satisfactory way. We need to make clear that our preference is for the action to stop early in good performance, not go on to result in discipline. Employees *can* understand that if we are careful in our approach.

Preventiveness

While it's sometimes necessary to discipline in order to correct unsatisfactory behavior—hence to punish the employee for that behavior—we should think of discipline as *preventive*, as much as possible. If we think only about what has happened in the past, even the immediate past, we fail to make full use of good disci- plinary principles. We have to deal with undesirable behavior. We can't just look the other way and forget what we've seen. But we can get some good mileage out of good discipline, espe- cially if we look to preventing behavior from occurring in the future. This applies not only to the disciplined employee but also to the other employees who have observed the entire pro- ceedings. They've seen the nonstandard performance and they've seen the results. If we've done our job well, they can see that standard performance is more acceptable than nonstandard —*to them*, as well as to us. A basic rule of thumb for handling any supervisory problem is that little problems are easier to han- dle than big ones. (A corollary to that is that little problems usually grow into bigger ones if left alone!)

Absence of Blame

Another characteristic of good discipline is that whatever action we take, whether corrective or preventive, we always direct our actions and thoughts and conversation with the employee toward *what* is right, rather than *who* is right. There are several reasons for this. First, if we deal with the action or the problem on a personal basis, trying to decide whether we're right or the employee is right, it becomes a matter of trying to win an argument rather than deal with performance. It's not our job nor purpose to pin the blame on somebody; we just want to do the right things by all concerned, *and get the job done properly*. For our part, the right thing is to see that we use good communications in giving instructions, provide ample training for the employee doing the work, make sure that the employee has all the tools required to perform the tasks assigned, and then provide the best possible supervision for that employee. If part of this supervisory action requires disciplining the employee (and we've made the rules and regulations plain, as well as the consequences for violation of these rules and regulations), then we do the disciplining, too.

The right thing on the part of the employee is to give a day's work for a day's pay, abide by the rules and regulations, and accept the responsibility for taking the resulting discipline when there is a violation. It means that the employees must feel some accountability for their actions and must face the job as something they're involved in all the way. If they see the job only as something they can do if they feel like it, then they will have a hard time accepting discipline. If they don't see that we are interested in doing the right thing, rather than finding somebody to blame or pick on, then they will constantly be trying to argue with us about our action. They'll always be trying to see how little they have to do to satisfy us, or how much they can get away with when we aren't looking. Note that these things are best established early, long before the employee is faced with discipline, because if we're having to deal with accountability at the same time we're dealing with discipline, our discipline is going to be much less effective.

Adequate Documentation

The next characteristic we want to deal with is often a thankless and tiresome one. It is that the action, behavior, or malpractice that brought about the discipline needs to be well documented. Documentation is tiresome, something we'd rather not do, and something we don't do well many times. We have to be sure to record the information in the proper way, with the proper notations and notifications. The employee needs to be aware of the documentation and it's purpose. We don't want to get in the position of trying to "trap" an employee. One easy way to learn to accept the time it takes to do good documentation is to view it as part of our job, not just a sideline of it. Most anything about good supervision takes time to do well. If we expect to be successful at doing a good job of appraising, it will take time (and some documentation). If we want to be sure an employee is well trained, then we will have to put in some time ahead of the training in planning, some time during the training, and some time following up on the training. Good training takes time, in other words, but it pays off, just like the time we spend in documenting the actions of employees when discipline is concerned. Where grievances are involved, they are often lost because of poor documentation, rather than because the employee wasn't guilty. This is a shame, and ruins much of our efforts in trying to get acceptable performance from our employees.

DISCIPLINE IS NO CURE-ALL

If we've been in supervision very long, we recognize that discipline is no cure-all for our people problems. To start with, by the time discipline becomes necessary, things aren't going very well. We're working on something that's out of phase with standards, work that's not being accomplished as it should be, and people who are violating our acceptable expectations. At best we can hope only to get things up to normal, and that will be difficult enough. Many times we won't succeed in solving the problem completely, and in addition we'll probably have some unhappy people on occasions. So be it! We have rules, people break the rules, we discipline, not everybody likes it. . . we still have to do our job in the best way we can. It's like one of our children who has done something requiring some punishment. They may not like it, they may pout and stomp around, even slam a door or two, but just because they make a scene is no reason for us to break the house rules. They get over it, and they're better for it. In the long run the respect they develop for us because we do have standards and expect them to be followed will more than offset whatever uneasiness we feel at the time of the discipline. But there are other side effects of discipline that aren't always good. Let's look at some of them.

Create Morale Problem

We've talked about the bad results we might get even if we do a good job on discipline. It's even worse when we don't do a very good job of disciplining. We wait too long, don't have our facts straight, fail to document as we should, get emotional with the employee, fail to give the employee any benefit of the doubt in uncertain things, attack the person's motives rather than behavior, and make it sound like it's the person we don't like rather than his or her behavior. If we're guilty of one or more of these when we exercise the disciplinary measures, we're going to have a problem, not only with that employee but with all who hear about it. There's not much we can do under such circumstances except try to do better next time.

Get a Reputation for Toughness

If we are consistent with our discipline, exercising it fairly and uniformly, people will respect us, but they may think of us as being "tough." As it happens, that's not all bad. If by "tough" they mean that we don't allow people to perform below the existing standards without our taking action they're right; and we deserve—and should be proud of—the reputation. More and more, we're beginning to see the need for some "toughness" (as opposed to ruthlessness or old-fashioned autocracy) to give the employees something to hold on to. In the last few decades we haven't been able to set very good bases to which they can anchor their respect. The schools, homes, and churches have sometimes failed to provide much stability for young people growing up, and the work place hasn't been as firm or as decisive as it should have been. In many organizations today the employees are searching for something to respect. If we create a good set of standards, expect people to hold to them, and deal decisively with those who don't, we will receive some well deserved respect. If toughness achieves these results, then things are in good shape!

Find Other Supervisors Inconsistent

Perhaps one of the biggest hazards we find in exercising discipline is inconsistency among supervisors. No matter how hard we try to be firm and go by the standards, we get into trouble because other supervisors in the same department or in the same organization somehow fail to follow the same set of rules. They are either too lenient or too strict, or in some way they differ from us in administering their discipline. To say the least, the results are hard on the organization, they are also hard on us as supervisors. Our people find it strange that we don't use the same set of standards or policies that they use, and they resent it when other supervisors let their people get away with things that would get them into trouble. Their people may gloat over the fact that their supervisor lets them do things the others don't. The resulting friction is hard on production and morale.

So, do we just quit employing any kind of discipline, become more or less strict, or what? The answer is obvious; we do the best we can at following the rules, trying to maintain as much consistency within our own operation as we can. That's all we can do as long as there is no effort within the organization to standardize all the supervisor's behavior under the same circumstances. There is one thing we find out as we supervise for awhile—no matter how poorly the rest of the organization is run, it is never a reason for us to be any less than the best supervisor possible.

We Over-Compensate for Our Discipline

Like our children, our subordinates sometimes try to give us some kind of "guilt trip" when we exercise discipline on them. They may say things to us, they may say things to others that we hear about, or they may get angry or pout. In some way they may end up making us feel guilty that we've suspended them, embarrassed them, or somehow made them feel uncomfortable. The *natural* consequence of this is for us to feel guilty. When that happens, we may do the worst possible thing and try to compensate by letting them get away with something they shouldn't, by doing them a favor such as letting them leave early or having some extra time at lunch, or maybe even by giving them some favoritism in job assignments. This wipes out the effect of the discipline, and creates more problems than we had before. Since one of the advantages of discipline is to set an example for other employees, over-compensating sets the wrong example and makes us wish we hadn't disciplined at all. So, no matter how badly the employee acts, or how bad we may feel, if we have done what we indicated we would under certain circumstances, we have to be *proud of ourselves* and go on.

Even if the employee doesn't like it, in the long run the other employees will respect us and will be better for it. It may take a few hours, or even a day or two, but it's worth the wait. A good rule is: never threaten to do anything we don't have the *authority* or the *fortitude* to carry out.

No doubt there are other consequences that make us wonder if discipline is really worth it, but we can be sure that unless the results are disastrous, we are better off to discipline when the situation calls for it. It's unfortunate that grown people have to be disciplined; it's too bad that all of our people don't do their job well and leave us to do our supervising in the best way we can. But that's not the way life is. We do have to see that people follow the rules, do their work, and meet the standards. There is some consolation, though. Almost everywhere that discipline is exercised fairly and properly, the need for it diminishes drastically! That in itself is reason enough to discipline when necessary!

CONCLUSION

There are other characteristics, perhaps, but these will set the stage for good disciplining. What we've tried to say is that good discipline is fair, unemotional, and should deal with what is correct, rather than dealing with individuals in a vindictive way. There are some rules and regulations for acceptable disciplining. While we've said that discipline should be done without emotion, we don't want to forget that the people we're working with are human beings who have feelings that should be respected. While we want to do what's right, rather than dwell on who's right, we make a diligent effort to look at previous work records, extenuating circumstances, and anything else we can consider without being unfair to either the person violating the organization's expectations or the other workers around this person. Finally, discipline is a tool of the supervisor, but that's all— just a tool, not a cure-all. Good supervisors use it just like any other tool—to keep things running as smoothly as possible in the long haul.

DISCUSSION ACTIVITIES

1. Why is it that many supervisors, both new and experienced, often avoid using discipline as a tool of supervision? *130*

2. What are some of the positive reasons why supervisors should make discipline a regular part of their supervisory role?

3. Discuss (debate) this statement: "No matter what the outcome, discipline always sets the supervisor-subordinate relationships back a few steps." *145-146*

4. List examples of inadvertently rewarding improper behavior and punishing desired behavior. *136*

5. List the characteristics of good discipline. *140-145*

6. Discuss (debate) this statement: "In discipline it's important to aim at *what's* right, rather than *who's* right." *144*

7. List alternatives to discipline and discuss their relative merits as compared to those of discipline. *131*

chapter 9

APPRAISING PERFORMANCE AND ASSESSING POTENTIAL

When we look at employees, we are really considering two things: first, how good they are at their present jobs; and second, how much potential they have for other jobs in the future. In other words, we must think of each employee as being actually two people. One is the person in the present job, with requirements or deficiencies, doing some things well and some poorly, needing much help or requiring little. The other is the person who might someday be able to do another job—a more complex job, a job of supervising people, a job of working with people or clients, or a job of working for long periods in silent concentration. We can't just look at this last employee and say that he or she is capable of doing thus and so right now. We have to consider what the employee could do with adequate *experience and training.* The first look we have we call *appraising;* the second look we call *assessing.* In this chapter we'll look at both processes, appraising and assessing.

WHY DO WE APPRAISE?

We said in an earlier chapter that employees need and deserve feedback on their performance. They need to know what they're doing well and what they're doing poorly. They need to be told this frequently so they can take advantage of their own abilities to improve without getting too entrenched in bad habits, and so they get the right amount of reinforcement when they do something well. So the employee needs to know where he or she stands (or falls down). But we as supervisors need that information, too. We need to be able to give a current, accurate appraisal of our employees whenever we're asked. Knowing these things about our employees is a part of the *controlling* function of any supervisor's job. Essentially, we control money, material, and human resources. If we know how well our people are doing, then we're at least doing a good job of that aspect of our work. Knowing our employees is also part of the *directing* function. Directing people requires that we know what they are doing and how well they are doing it so we can best direct their activities. Basically, appraising employees is just a function of supervision. As supervisors we are responsible for getting work done through other people, so we need to know how they're doing so we can see the extent of our success or failure at any given time.

Appraising is much like taking an inventory. It is an inventory of our human resources. Without reducing the significance of the employees, nor making them sound like nuts and bolts, we can make a favorable comparison between appraisals of people and physical inventories. We try to find out just what we have in stock. What do we have an ample supply of? What do we have an abundance of? What do we have a shortage of? How can we make what we have in stock do the job, and how can we use it to our best advantage? These are questions we ask about a materials inventory, and we need to know the same things about our people. We need to know what talent is plentiful, so we can take advantage of it and not get an oversupply by adding the wrong people. We need especially to know where the shortages are, because these will hurt performance. Then we need to know what we can do to best utilize the *existing* job capabilities, not the potential that may be out there somewhere in the future. We appraise to see what's happening right now, with the people we've got, doing whatever they're doing. The exciting thing about taking a human resources inventory is, as any experienced supervisor knows, that if we do our appraisal accurately and have a successful appraisal interview with our people, then we can get a *self-generating increase in stock*! That can never happen with our materials inventory.

WHAT DO WE APPRAISE?

Let's look at some rules of appraising. Most of these are obvious to the experienced supervisor, but it won't hurt to review them again.

1. The first rule of appraising is to appraise only those things that are *measurable and discernible.* Avoid appraising nebulous generalities like "attitudes," "loyalty," or "cooperation." If we're going to do this, we might as well go the rest of the way and measure love of country and thoughtfulness toward little children.

2. The second rule of appraising is to appraise *behavior.* This is the other side of the first rule, of course. Behavior is really all we've got a right to expect from an employee, since that's what we're paying for. We appraise what the employee is *doing* or *not doing.* That's all behavior is. That's all that is observable. If a smile is the behavior we're looking for, then we appraise the smile or lack of it, not "attitude" or "sincerity."

3. The third rule is to measure only those things the employee *has been trained to do,* or came to the job certified or qualified to do. When we measure things other than what the employee has been trained to do, we're really measuring potential. For example, if we say an employee doesn't write a very good letter, but the employee has never been trained in letter writing, then all we can justifiably say is that the employee will need training in letter writing before moving to a job requiring letter-writing skills. That's measuring *potential,* rather than existing skill, as we'll see later. However, if letter writing is a required skill on the existing job, and we haven't provided any training in this skill, then we're going to have trouble if we try to blame it on the employee. There's no way it can come out as a fault of the employee. (When we have the appraisal interview, we'd better have something definite in mind, too, in the way of training, because we can't just tell the employee, "You've got a real problem with your letter writing, and I'd like to see it improved by the time of the next ap-

praisal." We've got to offer the employee specific advice on *how* to improve his or her letter-writing skills.)

4. The next rule of appraising is always to measure against a *known standard*. We've all had the problem of doing an appraisal, finding an employee deficient in a certain area, and calling that to the employee's attention, only to be asked, "Just what exactly do you want me to do?" All at once it dawns on us that we don't really have an answer to the question. We don't like the performance and we want something better, but we don't know what it is "exactly." We end up trying to sound wise when we say, "Well, just let this be fair warning. I think you're smart enough to figure out what is expected of you around here." We ignore the puzzled look and go on to the next point. It's like the case of the boss who kept telling the employee that the letter prepared for the boss's signature wasn't quite right. After several attempts, each time getting the same response, the employee finally asked the boss just what it was that was wanted. The boss replied, "I can't tell you what I want, but I'll know it when I see it." That's operating in the absence of a standard!

There are other rules, perhaps, but these are the important ones. These are the ones that tell us what to look for in our appraisals and that will keep us out of the most trouble. Let's sum up the question of "What do we appraise?" by saying that *we appraise the behavior of the employee on the job for which he or she has been trained, measuring discernible actions against a standard that's known by both the supervisor and the subordinate.*

HOW DO WE APPRAISE?

Knowing how to appraise is much easier once we know why we appraise and what it is we're looking for in the appraisal. Remember, we've made a distinction between appraising and assessing. A little later in this chapter we'll see that we can actually do both of them at the same time—in fact, should do them both together—but for now let's keep them separate. The goal of our appraisal needs to be clear. We need to know not only what information we're looking for, but who is going to look at and use the information we find. Certainly we'll want to have it available for our own use and we'll want the employee to have access to our findings, usually during an appraisal interview. But who else will see and use the information? Those who've been around awhile know that funny things sometimes happen to appraisals. Sometimes they end up "upstairs," with people looking at them who hardly know the employee they are reviewing. There are even occasions where the results of the appraisals are changed by those above us or in another department, without our knowing why some of the decisions are made as they are. On rare occasions, the decisions on our appraisals are reversed or changed and *we may not even know it.* So we need to know who else is going to see the appraisals, even though we aren't always sure what they are going to do with them.

Let's discuss this matter of people changing our appraisals or using them in ways we don't approve of or understand. Does this mean that we really don't have to spend much time worrying about appraisals? Can we just slough them off, do them in a hurry, and get on to the more important things? Actually, many supervisors—even experienced ones—do just that. They say they've been around long enough to know that the appraisals are misused and so they don't waste time on them anymore. Is that a legitimate claim? No, not really. If we stopped putting effort into anything that somebody in the organization changed or did something to we didn't understand or like, we'd soon be out of a job. That's just a lazy excuse to keep from doing something that's often a very difficult task if done properly. It's no different from preparing a report or a project or a letter for the boss to sign or approve, knowing that there may be some changes, even though we won't approve of the changes. We should still do the job to the best of our ability, making the end product representative of our best effort. If it gets changed, that's someone else's prerogative; it's also somebody else's decision to live with. It's their accountability, not ours. Even so, we still have the responsibility to do that part of our job that has been assigned to us. If it's any consolation, remember that the better the job we do, the better chance our employees will have of coming out of the situation in good shape. If we do a poor job of appraising, not substantiating our findings, and then this poor appraisal goes to those who have less firsthand information than we do, then our employees are in bad shape. We're the only hope they have of getting fair treatment. If we don't do our work properly, they have no recourse. To that extent they're at our mercy.

Now let's look at the question of how we appraise. First, we appraise *over the whole appraisal period.* One of the problems supervisors have with appraisal plans is that appraisals are designed to be annual affairs, so the supervisors learn to think of appraising as something that happens once a year. Admittedly, the forms are often filled out once a year, but the *work* should be looked at all year, if that's the case. As we said earlier, even a not-so-bright employee can learn to look good the last several weeks before an appraisal in order to come out with a good report. There are a couple of reasons why this is so. First, we have short memories and when an employee is performing well the last several weeks before the appraisal we tend to enjoy it and forget about the less desirable behavior of earlier weeks. Secondly, we are all great ones for trying to encourage people to reform, and when we find an employee who is apparently turning over a new leaf we certainly don't want to discourage this behavior. So we end up giving the employee a good appraisal based on the last few weeks in which he or she is really showing signs of improving. The rest of the year—that time before the switch—the employee may have been performing quite poorly. Once we ignore that, or state that "the employee has shown remarkable improvement," *we're stuck with that appraisal for a whole year.*

Next we appraise *with the employee's assistance.* No matter what system the organization uses—what procedures, what forms, and who gets involved—unless it is expressly forbidden in the policy, be sure the employees provide their inputs into the appraisal activity. Most formal plans call for employee involvement, and we know it's a pretty good plan if that's the case. Regardless of what happens to the information—who changes it, sees it, files it, or whatever—if we've had a chance to sit down with the employees who work for us and talk about their performance over a period of time, then we've done a valuable thing. As we've said, even if the plan doesn't call for it, we should still find the opportunity to get together with the employees on a one-to-one basis.

APPRAISING, NOT FAULT-FINDING

When we have this confrontation, this getting together to discuss performance, we have to remember that our purpose is to →discuss strengths and weaknesses, not to point our finger and criticize bad performance. If there was ever a time in our relationship with our employees that we wanted to be calm and objective, as well as unemotional, this is it. Some supervisors use the appraisal time to try to straighten out an employee. They save up faults and irregularities, even things that should be a part of their disciplinary activity, and use the appraisal time to let the employee have it on all the bad things. If we've made anything clear in this chapter and others in this book, it's that we will be successful as supervisors only as long as we level with our employees about their poor performance at the time it happens. The chapter on discipline deals with this at great length, because it's a basic rule of discipline: deal with the deficiencies as near the time of their occurrence as possible. So we don't store up. We pick a time and meet with the employee to discuss performance. It's best if this isn't a surprise to the employee and if the employee has had some time before the meeting to think about his or her own strengths and weaknesses in the jobs being performed. Hopefully, somewhere there will be a meeting of the minds as to just what the employee is being appraised on. Some clarify this during the appraisal interview; some do it a week or two before; some ask the employee shortly before the interview to make a list of responsibilities and do an appraisal on each of these items. The better supervisors don't have to do this, because they've gotten that straight *at the time that the appraisal period started, whenever it was.*

Does there have to be agreement on the appraisal between the supervisor and subordinate? Not necessarily, although sooner or later disagreements need to be ironed out because they indicate a serious breakdown in communications. Either there is a misunderstanding of standards or a misunderstanding of how the employee is meeting those standards. There is little likelihood that jobs are going to be done satisfactorily if we can't agree with our people as to how well they're doing. Ideally, there would naturally be agreement because we've discussed progress and performance throughout the entire appraisal period. In fact, we may have looked at a certain trouble area sometime during the year, found a deficiency, suggested a remedy, then said that we would look at it again in a few months or at regular appraisal time. The only difference between a formal appraisal and the ones we do from day to day is that the formal one is much more comprehensive. Obviously we can't sit down every day and go over the person's entire battery of assignments and review each one of them. What we can do, though, is to see how work is progressing in the various work assignments *as they are happening*. At formal appraisal time, we can't do that.

When the employee comes in for the final review, whether or not there has been formal activity on his or her part, we conduct what is most often called an *appraisal interview*. Let's note a few important things about this interview. First, as we've said, it isn't an "unloading" session. To get an idea of what kind of atmosphere should prevail, *employees should look forward to their appraisal interview*. If we've done our preparation right—if we've let the employees know what is going on and had them working on their own appraisal—then they'll be ready, if not anxious, to come in. The manuals on how to conduct an appraisal interview always say to put the employee at ease with smalltalk before starting the interview. There's nothing wrong with that, but if we are making the interview that formal, and we don't have our employees into our office enough for them to feel at ease naturally, then we'd *better* make the smalltalk. As in any interview, the purpose should be stated at the beginning of the serious discussion. Once we've stated that purpose, we should be ready to launch into the interview. When the subject of appraisal comes up, then we ought to start doing just that, not reverting back to smalltalk. A good system for conducting the interview is to take one job responsibility at a time and go through it, with each person giving views on the strengths and weaknesses of the employee being appraised.

Now comes an important part of the interview. We've said

already that we appraise on observable and measurable behavior. When we are talking about performance and describing a strength or weakness, we should always be able to give an example, and as recent a one as possible. We can't just say, "You need some improvement in customer relations," or "You do a fine job of getting along with people." We need to be able to say, "You need to work on your customer relations skills some more. For example, the other day when . . . ," or "You should take advantage of your skill at dealing with people. The way you handled the situation with Fred the other day was a good example of your skill. As I saw it, what you did very well was. . . . " By giving examples we are able to pinpoint strong points so much better. And we want to avoid getting into an argument about a particular situation, which is all the more reason for having more than one example.

Supervisors who have a number of employees to appraise find it most helpful if they jot down examples of these things as the days go by. This will not only help at appraisal time, it will also help us to think back over the whole appraisal period. We might not use the older examples, unless we need to refresh the employee's mind or perhaps point out progress or deterioration in certain areas, but it is useful to have them available.

As the interview progresses, the supervisor can tell quickly whether or not the employee is getting uptight about the way things are going, or if the employee is accepting the things being said. Remember that people can accept the good things much better than the bad ones. This creates all the more reason to mix them together, rather than give all the good ones and then all the bad ones. If the interview isn't going well, *it's almost always our fault.* Somehow, we've been unable to keep things on an adult level. We may have let emotion get into it. We may have used the wrong tone in pointing out a weakness or trying to prove a point. Once we sense that the interview isn't going well, there are a couple of things we can do. One is that we can ease off, and be sure our voice is on a very even keel. A quiet voice is essential in keeping things calm. Then we can let the employee do more of the talking. Not arguing, but just talking, letting out feelings perhaps, saying things that we don't have to react to, taking over the conversation for awhile. We use those techniques they taught us in the old "talking with people" course. We nod or say, "I see," and let the employee keep on talking. We use reflective techniques, such as just turning the conversation back by repeating what the employee has just said without reaction, as in "You feel you have grown in this area, then. . . . " Or we can use open questions—questions that can't be answered yes or no—like, "What training do you think you need?" rather than, "You think you need some training?"

Using these techniques will usually get things back on a good footing, and things can proceed normally. From here on it's just a matter of being sure that all points are covered. It's essential that the employees leave with a clear understanding not only of what they're doing well and poorly, but also of what the plans are for correcting any weaknesses. We can be sure that the employee knows only when we hear the employee say these things, so we'd better be looking for as much feedback as possible. To do this we use the same techniques we talked about just now. *And we listen!* When we close the interview, these things should have been settled if they haven't been settled before:

1. What the employee's job responsibilities are
2. The standards for these responsibilities
3. How the employee is doing, both good and bad
4. What specific plans there are for improving the weaknesses and capitalizing on the strengths
5. The time frame for accomplishing the things planned

Now all we have to do is the necessary follow-up on the plans. That's much easier than the interview, because now we have agreement on the appraisal and on how to use the information gathered during the interview. We can pick up right there with the employee, at any time, and have a meaningful discussion.

ASSESSING EMPLOYEE POTENTIAL

When we start talking about potential, we're talking about something that's not nearly as definable as when we're talking of appraisals. We said that appraisals should be done in terms of *behavior* and *standards.* Those are essential in appraising, and are easily definable. In assessing, however, we're talking about how employees will perform in the future on a job for which they now have no responsibility, and for which they probably haven't been trained. We're trying to measure—and to a large extent predict—the future. This can be extremely tricky. So what do we do, go find a crystal ball and take it into a dark room and hope something shows up? In a way, it may sometimes seem as though that's what we're doing, but in fact it's a little more scientific than that. We'll see some things that will make assessing more accurate than mind reading or crystal ball gazing.

One of the problems we have in trying to assess potential is that we don't know what we're looking for. We look at an employee to see what the potential is, but we aren't looking for potential in any particular job or assignment. That's not unlike looking at a pair of pliers and asking, "I wonder how good that would be as a tool when I'm working on a car tomorrow?" The obvious questions are, What car? and Doing what on that car?

There are two ways to do an assessment. One is to look at the employee and get a profile of the strengths and weaknesses that now exist, and the other is to match the employee with the job.

Finding a Profile

You can get a profile of the employee's existing strengths and weaknesses from the appraisal. We can find out if the employee has interpersonal skills, can write letters, needs improvement in planning and organizing, and so on. Remember that this is a *profile,* meaning that each skill being considered exists to some extent. There's no such thing as a person who has *no ability* at letter writing, or planning, or dealing with others. Some may be very poor, some excellent, and most somewhere in between. The profile will tell us where in between, either on some kind of scale or with certain specified capabilities.

As we begin to develop our profile on each person, we start to get a clearer picture of those people's potential. It may even be that as we get a better look at them we may begin to see

"If I knew you were appraising me, then I'd know whether to just do an ordinary job, or to do something exceptional."

what other jobs they could fit into, perhaps with a little improvement in one area or another. We may even discover some talents and skills we missed during the appraisal, because in spite of ourselves, in an appraisal we invariably spot those things that are wrong or lacking more easily than those things that are good. This is especially important to watch when we start to think about future assignments. Since we're talking about things that may be useful on a different job, but may not be used at all on this one, we may not have even had a reason to look at these things during the appraisal period. We only looked at those talents and skills pertaining to the present job.

#7 Matching Employee with Job

We mentioned two ways of doing an assessment. One way is to look at the employee's total abilities without thinking in terms of a specific job. The other method is to think in terms of the next logical job the employee might progress to and then to see what the person's capabilities are for this particular job. This becomes a simple matter of matching an employee with an existing job, and that's much easier than the first method. We ask ourselves, "What does the job require?" and then see which of these requirements the employee can or cannot fulfill. Here again, though, we have to be careful, because we want to look at standards, not just the need for a certain skill. If manual dexterity is required, we need to know *how much,* since every worker has some amount of dexterity. Does it have to be enough dexterity to handle very small objects without misusing them? Does the employee need to be able to do tedious work for long periods of time without getting tired or frustrated? These are better standards than just "manual dexterity." The same is true for any job we're talking about. For example, "A need for customer relations skills" is pretty nebulous. How much skill? What kinds of skills? What kinds of customers? How many customers in a day? The answers to these kinds of questions will give us a much better standard to go on than if we just give the job responsibilities. Notice what happens when we begin to examine the standard in detail, and compare the prospective filler of that job. We end up with the *training needs* for the individual. We have, in fact, done a *needs analysis* as far as this person being able to fill the job. We may not ever go through with the program, since the employee may not be headed for that job. But if we do expect the person to fill that vacancy, we'll have to train the person in the things we've found deficient. Otherwise, we'll have a person with a known deficiency filling the job, and then we'll be where we are when we appraise an employee and find inadequacies. If we aren't careful, we'll end up blaming the employee, not ourselves.

We should notice here that if we use the second approach to assessing, matching a job and the person, we end up with a pretty definite training program if we desire to pursue it. If we use only the profile method we may or may not get a good training needs analysis. The problem with this method is that we end up with a list of weaknesses, many of which won't make any difference on some jobs the individual might get. If we train on all the skills, we may end up with an "overtrained" person, who may not ever use all this training! This would indicate that we should find out what the person is likely to do before assessing that person, but it has the drawbacks we mentioned. How can we decide which method to use? The answer is easy *if* we know fairly well what the person will be doing in the next job. In many cases this is already determined. The person in sales will most likely stay in sales; the person in office management will probably stay there; the accountant, the engineer, the clerk-typist, all have a path that is obvious for a while, at least. It's the ones who may be likely to move from one job to another who will give us trouble.

This leads us to another consideration, though one we won't spend much time on. This is a matter of career planning. While there are some dangers in doing it (we may lock a person into a path that isn't really the right one), it certainly works well here. If we've got a career plan for the individual being appraised, all we have to do is look at it and see what the next job requires. From this we have our standard; we do the assessment in terms of this standard, find what additional development is required, and decide when and how this development will be done.

Finding Unseen Talents

None of what we've said so far takes into consideration that we have employees working for us who have all kinds of potential that is unknown to us (and to the employee, in many cases). When a present job does not require use of a particular skill, we have no opportunity to observe the skill in action. If the job doesn't require leading conferences, how will we know if the person has potential in that area? If the job doesn't require extensive contact with disgruntled employees or customers, we won't know, *from watching the employee on the present assignment*, whether there is already a talent there, or if it could be developed. It's fine if, by watching a person perform a minor task, we find that this same skill could be developed into a very valuable skill with some training and development. But think what a great thing we have done if we discover a talent or skill that wasn't being used, but could be of great value to the organization—a skill that even the employee didn't know was there! We have to be alert to discover these kinds of things.

What are some of the ways we find these undiscovered skills? Sometimes just by luck. We see an employee in a different setting than usual and suddenly recognize a skill that could be developed into a useful one on some future job. It may be during a discussion in which the employee takes over the organization's argument and convinces the other employees. It might be in connection with an employee activity, such as organizing an employee ball team or a social activity of some kind. Perhaps we hear that the employee has been active in a civic group, taking a lead in some action, without thinking about it as involving a job-related skill. Perhaps we see a letter the employee has written to the governor or congressperson, and realize the letter did a good job of summing up the problem in very concise terms. Maybe we see the employee operate in a crisis of some kind, say a production schedule that is about to be missed, and we watch as the employee tackles the problem in a systematic way, using good organization and planning skills. As we have said, sometimes this is accidental. But as we'll see next, these things could be discovered on purpose, with a little planning.

Finding Skills on the Job

We really aren't too happy about finding that employees have skills only *if we're lucky*. There must be a more systematic way. There is, and it's pretty obvious to those who've been around for a while as supervisors. In fact, for most good supervisors it's a natural way of life for them. The idea is to simply build into the job ways of checking on the hidden talents of our people. If they don't have to do the things that we think the next job will require, then we make arrangements for them to try some of these things. This involves both training and assessing, and we should remember that. If we want to know how well an employee might organize a job, but the present job doesn't really give much chance for using organizing skills, then we allow the employee to work on part of our work that does require it. No, we don't give the employee all the job all the time. We pick a part of the assignment that looks like it will have a little planning in it, explain the task to the employee, then turn it over to the person. We can watch as closely as possible, because this is different from the ordinary delegation. We aren't trying to see how well the employee takes delegation, we're trying to see how well the employee plans an assignment.

Remember, the employee may need some guidance and training to do this. We're not only interested in seeing if the skill is already there; we also want to know if the employee can learn it if it isn't. This means that we must be willing to spend some time in training. The most practical way is to give only a small portion of the planning task to the employee the first time, and then allow more and more, watching to see just how much training is required with each larger step. If we see that a great deal of training is going to be required, we're beginning to get our answer already. Since we're not trying to get the employee to actually take over the job, it isn't necessary for us to continue until the employee becomes completely proficient. We just want to know whether there's potential there, and this is one way of finding out.

Does the employee know that we're testing for potential? By all means! After all, we want to be able to sit down with the employee later on and explain the profile we've built, and if we're going to be looking at some area of the performance, the employee ought to know what it is, and why. In fact, we should make it clear to the employee that *this isn't a part of the regular job.* If we don't, and the employee fouls up in some way, then we're going to have an unhappy worker on our hands. Suppose we tell the employee we're trying to find out what potential exists, and the employee still falls on his or her face. Won't we get the same dissatisfaction? Yes, there will be some, but we can head it off in a couple of ways. First, we can point out that it will be good for both of us to find out what potential exists, and that there are many areas where all of us need much improvement. We can point out further that until we find out where our shortcomings are, we can't really grow. Just finding out what we can *do* doesn't give us room to grow. Spotting a deficiency gives us a target to shoot at, a goal to achieve, something to learn. The second thing we can do to head off the dissatisfaction is to keep giving the employee different kinds of jobs. As we give more and more different kinds of assignments, the employee will succeed in some and fall short in others. One failure won't be as obvious.

Are there really this many different kinds of assignments? Won't I spend all my time just thinking up assignments to give to people? Well, maybe and maybe not. Now we *can* talk about delegation. In our normal routine of supervising, we should just naturally find many things that can and should be delegated. In fact, good supervisors constantly operate on the premise that they should never do anything an employee under them could do. It's the old, "Getting the job done through other people" we talked about in the first chapter. When we're gone from the job, for example, we usually leave someone on the job as acting supervisor. What better time to find out all kinds of things about a person's potential? *But this works only if we design the assessing into the acting supervisor's role.* To just go off and leave the person in charge without planning any specific things to look for when we return isn't going to get the job done. Of course, we're interested in how well the employee handles the whole job, but we need to use such opportunities as chances to learn some specific things. We might want to check the person's ability to work with other departments, so we say, "While I'm gone, see how far you can get in working with personnel on the new computerized record system. They're putting some pretty close deadlines on us, and maybe they're justified. You don't have to get it settled—just see what you can find out. We want to cooperate in any way we can." If we want to, we can go a step further and say, "This will be a good chance for you to test your ability to work with another department. Coordination is a constant part of some jobs, and this requires a certain amount of skill. Let's talk a little about how to go about dealing with them. . . ." Now we go into a training program of sorts so the employee will have some elementary skills to take to the task. After all, this is the real world, and we aren't just playing at coordination. We want a job done, and we're giving it to a subordinate to do. We aren't giving up the responsibility—we still share it in the long run, however it comes out. When we return, we can go over the assignment, do our assessing, and have some reliable data to go on as far as the employee's potential is concerned.

CONCLUSION

So there we have it. A look at appraising and assessing—two different things to look at in the same employee. Neither is easy. Both require practice and skill. Both are necessary if we expect to do our jobs properly. If we do well at them, we've done favors for the organization, ourselves, and the employees. If we do a bad job, everybody suffers, including ourselves. We're costing the organization money and time any time we don't see our employees in the proper light, even if they aren't as good as we think they are. We need to know that. the organization needs to know that, and certainly the employees need to know that. There shouldn't be any secrets at appraisal time, though. We should keep our employees appraised and apprised all along as to how they're doing. At appraisal time, we're just documenting what should already be known and understood between us and our people.

DISCUSSION ACTIVITIES

1. What is the difference between *appraising* and *assessing* employees? #150

2. Discuss (debate) this statement: "The first rule of appraising is to appraise only those things that are discernible and measurable." #150

3. Why is it that many experienced supervisors come to regard appraisals as having little or no value? Discuss the validity and fallacies of this belief. #154

4. Discuss (debate) this statement: "Employees don't need to be told how they're doing—after all, they know their own strengths and weaknesses." #156

5. Why is it that employees often dread appraisal sessions?

6. What part does luck play in finding potential in employees? How dependable is it?

7. How can we tell if an employee has the potential for a job when he or she isn't doing that job now?

8. How essential is it for us to be accurate in our assessment procedures? What kind of impact do bad decisions in assessments have on the organization?

chapter 10

PREPARING FOR THE NEXT JOB

The experienced supervisor is often seen as being in a rut, without ambition, or any real desire for the challenge of a promotion. In reality, there is little to substantiate that idea. On the contrary, there is much to indicate that ambition rarely dies; it just becomes suppressed to prevent the bitterness that accompanies nonpromotion and nonrecognition. This isn't to say that someone who has been on the job awhile is automatically a failure—far from it. It does suggest, though, that if we are interested in promotion or movement within the organization, we should do certain things toward that end. In this chapter we'll look at some of those things.

WHERE ARE WE NOW?

There is a legend that says that when someone asked Daniel Boone if he had ever been lost, he replied that he hadn't, but that he was confused once for several days. The same can be said of many experienced supervisors. They say they know where they're going, but when it gets right down to it, they have trouble figuring out where they are right now. There are three ways to be lost. The first, and most common, way is when we don't know *how* to get where we're going. We know where we are, and we know where we're going, but we don't know how to get from here to there. This is not too serious a problem, however, because there is usually someone who can help us find the way. If we're lost in the second way, when we don't know where we're going, we're in trouble because no one can help us very much. An old Hindu proverb suggests that "If you don't know where you're going, any road will get you there" (or, as the seamen say, "Any wind will do!"). But there is a third way to be lost that is more frustrating yet. This is when we don't know where we *are right now.* This is the kind of confusion Daniel Boone was talking about. It's the kind of confusion that haunts many supervisors after they've been around awhile. They aren't sure just where they are right now.

How does this come about? How does it happen that we work hard, satisfy those above us enough to be promoted to supervisor, then gradually find ourselves drifting without much purpose? The reasons are certainly varied, but one of the main ones is that we unconsciously lose sight of just where we stand at any given time. We need to update ourselves periodically. We need to find out just where we stand with the organization. We may find this out in appraisals, but if we don't, we should make every effort to get the answer from our boss. We shouldn't ask in a threatening or demanding way, but in the matter-of-fact way we request any vital information. We need to find out how we're seen by those above us. Are we acceptable? Below standard? Above average? Even more important, just how are we seen as far as our day-to-day energies are concerned? Are we seen as wasting time on useless pet projects, or devoting our time in efficient ways? Are we seen as someone top management can rely on, or as just another body without much to contribute to the day-to-day decision-making process? Are we seen *right now* as being able to handle more people, make higher-impact decisions, and accept more responsibility, or are we seen as having the *potential* to do these things? Part of finding out where we are includes seeing if we *like* what we find out. If we do—that is, if we agree—then we're ready to move on to the next phase of our development. If we don't agree with what we find out about how we're seen by those above us, then we have to do something about that before we can move on.

Is it possible to change our image? It's not easy, but it *is* possible. Later in this chapter we'll see how to overcome those obstacles that stand in the way of our getting where we're going, and one of them is our present image. It's not likely that we'll be seen as having much potential for the next job if we're not seen as doing the present job in a satisfactory way. If we've developed the present image over a period of time, it will take at least the same period of time to change it, unless we're more successful than most or are able to do some rather spectacular things with our present job functions. As we'll see later, though, it's important that we start making this change as soon as possible, because the longer we wait the more change will be necessary.

There's another consideration here. If we don't like our present image (the image that higher management has of us) then we should also face the possibility that *there's some truth to the image.* Of all the analyses we have to do, self-analysis is the hardest. Getting a good, clear picture of ourselves is difficult, if not downright impossible. If we think that prejudices get in the way of our understanding others, that's nothing compared to what our prejudices will do to our ability to get a clear view of our own capabilities, strengths, and weaknesses. And again, although we've mentioned that the appraisal is the time for this to come out, we don't have to wait until then to discuss our performance with our boss. Any time we have questions we should take the opportunity to check out our feelings with top management. This doesn't mean we run in and out of the boss's office every few minutes, saying "How am I doing?" However, when we've finished a project of some magnitude, or completed an assignment that required the use of many managerial skills, that's a good time to ask for a review. Under ideal circumstances, we can thus have the boss looking at us (developing a changing image, perhaps) right after we've finished doing a good job. If we didn't do such a good job, at least we'll find that out too, and hopefully find out why. Certainly we'll need to know why if we're ever going to change our image and grow to the next assignment.

WHERE DO WE WANT TO BE?

Now we come to the next phase of finding ourselves. After we've found out just where we are, and have worked out a process for changing our image for the better (if it needs it), then we have to decide where we are trying to get to. Not just in terms of one promotion, but in terms of what we want to be doing in the years to come, and setting some goals for ourselves. As we'll see, it's a little dangerous to try to set rigid goals for ourselves in most cases, but we should at least have a rough idea of what we'd like to be doing two years from now, five years from now, and perhaps even ten years from now. We should also allow for the possibility that we'd like to be *right where we are now!* There's nothing wrong with that. In fact, it would do most of us good to get in that frame of mind because nothing can make a job more miserable than to think of ourselves as failures because all we've done is stay on our present job for a long time. If we like it, are well-accepted on it, know it, and do it well, and there is still more that we can contribute and learn, then we'd be foolish to think of moving just because we've been there for a long time.

The process of determining where we want to be includes several phases. First, we have to decide the kind or *type of work* we want to be doing. Are we satisfied with our present kind of work, or are we interested in changing to some other kind of work within the organization? (Here we have to be careful, of course, because the grass gets greener when it grows in somebody else's shop!) If we're satisfied that we're in the right area of work, then our decision is simply one of moving up or staying where we are. There is not the problem of figuring out how to get into another department or taking training for another field of work. We simply direct ourselves toward getting what we want in our own department, group, or specialty.

The next action is to decide *how far* we want to go. It's ridiculous for us to say "all the way" if we realize that's not possible. On the other hand, if we see no reason why we can't hit the top, then by all means we should set our sights in that direction. It helps to be honest with ourselves, but we shouldn't apologize for ambition. There's always opportunity for us to grow in most organizations, so growing into the next job or an expansion of our present one is a legitimate ambition. As we'll see later, we make both short- and long-range plans for moving on with our career, so we have to take into consideration how far we want to go and when we hope to be there.

All of this brings us to the point that career planning is a fragile hope in most cases. The truth is, very few of us ever get to where we plan on getting, and even then we often end up not really wanting to be there after all. This should in no way prevent us from making plans, though, for it is in the carrying out of these plans that other things happen. People see us working on one assignment (which *we* think is going to be on our record to get us to some pre-planned destination) but it may also be that they are impressed with our ability to write or speak or manage a certain kind of people, and make us an offer of promotion or change on the basis of that. The actual project may even go unconsidered. Remember, though, if we hadn't been *doing something,* nothing would have come from the situation.

Finally, we have to decide *how long we want to take* to get where it is we want to go. This is just as nebulous as the rest, of course, but we can get some general ideas. In fact, we can decide if we're willing to wait as long as we think it may take, and if this seems too long we change our goals. How do we determine how long it will take us? Since most crystal balls are tarnished and cracked, we don't have a ready source of help in this area. There are some things we can do, however. We can look at others with the same background, experience, training, skills, aptitude, and so forth, and see how they progressed as far as time is concerned. Assuming the organization is relatively similar now, this will help us some. In the long run, most promotions and transfers average out. Look at a number of people and see what their movement rates average out to. This will give us some kind of target information, if not anything too specific. There are other considerations, such as the possibility of movement within the organization above us. What kind of reorganization plans are under consideration? How does our boss figure into this organization? How do we fit into it? Admittedly, all of this may be speculation, but as long as we don't forget to do our present job while we think about it, there's no real harm done.

We have to consider something else here as well. Time often works for us, but it can also work against us. It works to discourage us. It works to make us bitter. It works to cause us to wonder if we're ever going to make a move again. It's a good idea for us to look at an organization chart every once in a while. The usual progression for most people is to move faster in the early years, then less rapidly as time goes on. This may cause us to wonder if we're slipping behind. The organization chart will answer this for us. In the beginning there are more jobs at the next level above us, and even though there are more people for those jobs, there are other influences such as turnover, people leaving for other departments, and more incompetence. These things make it possible for competency to be easily spotted *and rewarded.* As we move up in the organization, though, these things are no longer true. There are fewer and fewer jobs above us, and the competition is much greater. The people around us are more stable, more competent, more career oriented, and more likely to have the same goals as we do. All of this makes it harder for us to move ahead, combined with the fact that the jobs above us are more difficult and require more experience to fill. We just have to determine in our minds that our movement will be slower, and that the slowness will leave us better prepared in the long run.

WHAT STANDS IN MY WAY?

The next logical step after we've decided where we are and where we want to go is to decide what stands in our way of getting there. We've just mentioned some of the things: the competition (those who want the same things we want), the boss, and the bosses above our boss. These do get in our way, of course, but they are not what we want to consider here. What we want to think about has more to do with ourselves and those things we can control. For example, we must consider *our own job performance.* We've been discussing the need for taking a long look at ourselves to see just how we shape up. If we don't like all that we see, then this is one of the things we can do something about. We've even seen in this chapter some of the things we can do.

We also have to look at that next job. Perhaps we are doing a satisfactory job where we are. Perhaps we're considered as having potential, even some good skills for the next job. But it would be hard to imagine that we're *completely* qualified for the next job. What we need to do is get a profile of our strengths and weaknesses, hopefully through a good appraisal system, and then start to work on the weaknesses. If we have trouble running a meeting, or writing a report, or speaking before a group, or organizing our work, or doing long-range planning, or solving problems, or making decisions, or delegating work, or training subordinates, or any of a number of managerial skills that we may be required to handle at the next level, then we need to start to improve on these things *right now*. It may mean taking outside courses at night, or attempting to get into an organizationally sponsored course, and if so, we should take the necessary steps to get into these courses. It may mean that we will have to improve these things right on the job, and if so, we should look for opportunities to do so.

It is time here for a word of caution. We need to be sure that we're practicing the right things, and practicing them correctly. Practice at doing things poorly will only make us *better at being bad*. We need to study our weaknesses, find out what we're doing incorrectly, and then find out what the correct behavior is so we can practice good performance rather than bad. We also need to keep sharpening our good skills. The fact that we do some things well may indicate natural tendencies in these areas, and if that's so we want to keep getting better in these areas too. We probably can grow faster in the areas where we have natural talents. Interestingly enough, because we can probably get more recognition in those areas where we're already doing well than in those where we need improvement, we tend to ignore the areas where we do poorly. However, if we spend all our time developing our lesser talents, then we may not get recognized for the good things we can already do. For this reason we must be sure to keep on doing the things we do well—developing them, getting seen doing them, getting even better at them—at the same time as we work on our weaknesses.

While we're looking at obstacles that stand in our way, let's think again about the competition. While we don't want to think about playing games with people, or trying to undermine others, it's well to see what talents *they* have. These talents, if needed in the job above us, or in the job we aspire to, are in our way in the sense that they exist in others but not in ourselves. Rather than run them down, we do as we do in any kind of fair competition: we try to get better ourselves. We sharpen our skills in those areas where others are ahead of us, at the same time as we use the skills we're good at to keep us in the forefront. We keep repeating ourselves here, but let's note that we should avoid thinking that there is just one job for us to aspire to, or that the person chosen will always come from right here in our work group. This certainly happens sometimes, but it's not the rule by far. At the same time, we keep our hands clean by doing the present job well, learning for the future, and being willing to sit back and let the future take care of itself, as we'll see later.

A PLAN OF ATTACK

So here we are. We've found out where we are now, where we want to go, and what stands in our way. Now how do we get there? This process too consists of many steps. We look at those things that we do well, and consciously do them as well as possible. That's a short-term process. We pay careful attention to appraisals, wanting to hear as much as possible about our strengths and weaknesses. We don't spend time defending ourselves or feeling sorry for ourselves because we're misunderstood. We listen to our present image, determine what we want to change about it, *then get started*. (It's the getting started that's important.)

There are long-range plans, too. Where do we need improvement? Once that's determined, we can't just wave a wand and change overnight. Even if we have skills in these areas but just aren't using them, we have probably developed some bad habits. These habits will be hard to change, and correcting them will probably have to be a part of our long-range planning. If we're not in the habit of delegating work to lower levels, for example, it won't come to us *naturally* for a long time. We'll have to consciously do it for a good while, reminding ourselves that we need developing in this area. We will know that we have become proficient in this area when we discover that *without thinking about it*, we've delegated something that we used to do ourselves.

Further, we should let it be known that we desire to grow

"What do you mean you want my job—and what are you doing on the seventh floor—and who are you?"

and move in the business. Expressing ourselves as being ambitious shouldn't hurt us, especially if we don't put the boss on the spot by saying something like, "I want that next opening, and nothing is going to stand in my way of getting it!" This sounds too much like a threat. What we do say is, "I want to grow as much as possible, and contribute as much to the organization as I can." This means that we aren't aiming at a particular job as much as trying to develop to fit many jobs before it's over. We don't make a constant issue of this, by the way. Appraisals are a good time to discuss our hopes and aspirations. We're already talking to the boss about the strengths and weaknesses of our performance in our present job, so we can simply expand the discussion into the future. Many good appraisal systems have this built into them already, so we may not have to bring up the subject. When we know we're going in for a discussion with our boss at appraisal time, this is a good time to get ourselves together about the future as well as the present. We'll be ready to discuss it, regardless of who brings it up.

Finally, let's be reminded that what counts the most is what we're doing right now. In the long run, promotions or moves will more likely be made on the basis of our present performance than on the basis of all the other factors put together. If we do the self-analysis we've talked about here, then set a plan for ourselves, we also go to work and make sure our existing job is well covered. This is when we make sure we're meeting standards and more. We make sure we are doing imaginative things and innovative things, where these are called for, and we make sure we are doing things very much by stated policy when this is called for. We make sure we don't lose our opportunity for moving on by letting the present job slip while we dream of the next great assignment we're planning to have!

WHO AM I?

One thing that is very interesting about looking into the future is that often we aren't really sure where we are right now! There's an interesting story about a man who was lost, and everytime somebody tried to tell him where to go, he would get more lost. Finally he told everybody to quit trying to help him until he figured out where he was right then. He reasoned that the only way he could ever get "unlost" was to decide just where he was, so as he could have some reference point from which he could continue. There's a lot of truth in that as far as our own lives are concerned. Many people don't necessarily like where they are, but they haven't stopped to figure out just what it is they don't like and where they'd like to be instead. Life is full of waiting for something to happen. We can't wait until we're old enough to go to school, then we can't wait to get to high school, then college. We can't wait to get out of college so we can get a job; we can't wait to get married and have children; then we can't wait until they go to school, get out of school, get married, and move away from home so that we can have more privacy and independence. Then we can't wait to retire, and finally find ourselves getting all of our enjoyment out of looking back, many times at what could have been if we'd just *lived instead of waiting to live.*

What's the problem? We are so busy looking to the future that we don't see the present very well. We aren't really sure what we like and don't like; we aren't sure who we really are or what our priorities are. We work, go home, eat, see the family, watch television, go to bed, wake up, and go to work, and then we're right back repeating the day before, the week before, the month before, the year before . . . and on and on. We aren't going anywhere, but that's all right because we don't really know where we'd like to go. The first thing we need to do is get a good look at ourselves. If we really want to find out, here's a good way to do it.

First, take a bunch of 3 x 5 cards, or pieces of paper about that size, and write all the things we are, each on a different card. For example, I may be a mother or father at the same time I'm a son or a daughter, so on one card I might have "Mother" or "Father" and on another I would have "Daughter" or "Son." I may be a supervisor, I may be a model-airplane builder, I may be a believer in God, I may be a student in night school, I may be a member of a lodge, and I may be a little league coach—all at the same time. In other words, I can be many things at the same time. We should list all of those things on different cards.

Next, I begin the difficult task of ranking the things I am in the order of their importance to me, with the most important first and the least important going toward the back of the stack. It will be hard, but remember that, just as we are many of those things at once, we can stop being any of them at anytime. If I'm a husband, my wife could die or I could get a divorce. If I'm a parent, my children could be killed. I could lose my job, give up my hobby, and lose interest in the lodge. So I ask myself, "Which of these come before the other in my life?"

Then, just as we did before, I begin taking cards out of the stack. Presumably, I'd start at the back and work my way to the front, but it may not work that way. I ask myself, looking at all of these cards, "Which would I keep ahead of everything else?" Gradually, I work the cards down to the last three or four—no more. When I get the cards down to these few, I have established my priorities. I have answered the question, "What's important to me now?" For the time being, at least, *I know who I am.*

We may be surprised at what we keep and what we choose to discard. Remember, discarding a card doesn't mean it isn't important, it means that if it comes to a choice of giving up one or the other, one is *more* important. That's what priorities are all about—deciding what comes first in our lives. We do have to make choices and we do have to give up some important things in our lives in order to do more important things.

Now that we've seen where we are, as far as priorities are concerned, we must make a decision about whether we do or do not like what we discovered. We may not like the idea that our career comes ahead of our family, or that our hobby comes ahead of religion, or that my going to school is more important *at this time* than my spouse. But if that's the way it is, then we should decide to like it or change it. On the other hand, if we decide we like the priority as it is and something comes ahead of the job, we have to face the fact that it will be harder for us to progress in our jobs as long as something else gets first choice of our time and energy.

There's *nothing wrong* with something coming ahead of my job. I just have to accept the fact that I will progress only in keeping with the energy, thought, and time I put into it. By the same token, if my job comes ahead of the family, I shouldn't be surprised if family problems develop which I can't cope with very well. The important thing is that when we finally understand what we are, we need to accept it and decide it's what we want. Only when we do accept it, can we begin to move on to something else. Liking ourselves becomes the key to doing good things *for* ourselves!

MY LIFE LINE

There's another exercise that will help us understand not only who and what we are and the priorities in our lives, but also where we're going and what we're likely to be doing in the future.

First, we pretend that some movie company is going to make a movie of our life. They've asked us to make a script for them to use, and they want it to be as near to the facts as possible. They'd like it to be in chronological order, preferably with the key events pointed out in some kind of time line. Our job is to decide what's important enough in our life to be in the movie (things like athletic events, honors, graduations, marriage, family events, jobs, promotions, education, etc.), and then decide what other characters we want to include (because they are important to us).

The easy way to do this is by listing the events, the times, and the characters, then making a scaled time line and inserting these things on it. Having done this, we now need to study it and decide when things have happened in our lives.

Have most of the key things happened lately, or some time ago? Were there more when we were young, so that now we find ourselves in a rut . . . or do we see our lives being filled with more and more important events. Is there a trend in the key events; are they getting better or worse? When I use the last few years as my trend-guide, do I like where things are headed? If, by projecting this line, I determine where I'm likely to be five years from now (based on the trend of events in the past five years), do I like what it tells me? Will I be where I'd like to be five years from now? Is there anything happening lately in my life that is different from what was happening five to ten years ago? Does this tell me anything about where I'm headed? Let's assume that the movie has been made and that the story of our life was such a hit the same company comes to us for a sequel . . . this time projecting into the future so we don't have to deal with just the facts.

This time we have more control over what goes into the movie. Before we could control only the selection of what we wanted to reveal from events that already happened with characters as they really interacted with us. This time we are dealing with fiction, so we can make our lives what we want them to be and can include any kind of people we want. We attempt any career, get any job, be any place, live any way, and have any financial situation we desire. The only restrictions on us are our own lack of imagination and our own conservative approach to things. The only thing we can't do is draw a time line because we don't know when death is going to appear on the scene.

This is a critical exercise, for even though it is fiction, it tells us that our restrictions are mostly mental. We are our own biggest barrier to being what we want to be. Usually, we don't think of being somebody, doing something, or making certain friends because we simply say, "Oh well, I could never do that." With the wipe of a mental stroke, we do away with our opportunities. Our ability to do this exercise, adding things that are imaginative, and fun, and exciting, will tell us about the likelihood of our actually accomplishing anything much different in the years ahead. It will also tell us if we are going to spend the rest of our lives just waiting for the time to come when something different happens. It certainly isn't any kind of psychological test, and there's no norm for the results, but it will tell us about our willingness to think beyond our present lifestyle with regard to both doing new things and establishing new relationships.

Many people save for a lifetime, planning, reading, and dreaming, about taking a trip or a cruise. Finally at retirement they are able to do it. They go and it meets all their expectations. Until they die they will remember that trip, talk about it, look at the pictures, and be quite happy that they went. Others think about a trip like that and immediately write it off as a dream, "I'd never be able to make a trip like that." And they never do. But there is a third group of people who think about how much fun it would be to travel to various places but don't want to wait until they retire. They want to go now. And they do.

What's the difference? These three groups have three different viewpoints. One is able to dream, plan, and have the patience to do a once-in-a-lifetime thing. They knew what they wanted to do and did it, even though they limited their thinking to one trip and probably sacrificed some other traveling to save for it. They were proud that they were able to prove they could do it, and it was quite a feat for them.

A second viewpoint, is represented by the people who simply washed the whole thing out, though they'd really have liked to make the trip. They had severe limitations on what they perceived themselves as being able to accomplish. They had as much opportunity, money, time, and ability to travel as the first group, but they lacked the imagination to plan something they wanted to do and the "expansion" of thought to see themselves actually engaged in making the trip. There's a good chance they have also failed to accomplish much else that has stretched their imagination.

The third group is the most interesting one. With the same amount of time, money, and ability, they ended up making more than one trip. They did it while they were younger, and they had many more memories when they were older. They had things to look forward to because they didn't make just the one trip, and the other trips were to different places they wanted to visit. These are the same people who go skiing, write books, learn to play the piano, go rafting down the white water streams, and whose imagination isn't limited. "Hey, wait a minute," somebody says. "I don't want to go anywhere or write any books, and I'm certainly not interested in riding rafts down some crazy river or killing myself skiing!" Perhaps this represents yet another group. Again, there's nothing wrong with not wanting to do these things. One isn't cast out of society because they don't have the urge to travel or have adventure, but it does restrict their right to be dissatisfied with their present lot in life! They have set their own life style and have no interest in anything different, hence they must accept what they have. If they are content to do their job, go home and spend a few hours with the family, watch television, and go to bed, then they may have the potential to be the happiest of all the groups. The problem is that they must learn to be content in that environment, and not envy or criticize others who go places, do things, and lead what might be called "exciting" lives.

So, where are we? We were doing a lifeline for the second "future," part of our lives. We found that, for the most part, the restrictions were built into us, not into our surroundings. It is this same way on the job. How would we make assignments of new and different kinds of jobs to the groups we've mentioned? To which group would we assign a job that requires some breaking from tradition and the use of imagination? Would we give it to the group that only had one plan and felt they could make only the one big splash in their lives? If for no other reason than that they would make too big a project out of it, we probably wouldn't give it to them. Neither would we give it to the second group who thought the first group was crazy for trying something new, nor to the last group who were completely satisfied with things just as they were. None of these groups would have the initiative to take on a project that might suggest that the old way of doing things is no longer the best way.

The group that has done things—has sort of "beat the odds"—is the group most likely to be able to take a project and run with it without having it overwhelm them. They wouldn't be as likely to make such a big operation out of it that the time and effort expended on it would make it unworthwhile. At the same time, they would give the project some initiative and imagination and would not be frightened if the solution might be one that had never been tried before. Sometimes we might have to temper their solutions down, but that's all right—at least we have something with which to work. With the other groups we would most likely find their solution looking very much like all the other solutions—though that is not always bad.

By the way, there's a place for all the groups; we also need steady people who can do the same job the same way and give it the benefit of their experience. Again, the question is, "Which do we want to be?" We have within us the power to choose. We can make the right choice after we've decided who we are and where we want to go.

CONCLUSION

Getting ready for the next job is a well-defined process in which we have to make some decisions about ourselves. We have to know where we are, where we want to be, and what is keeping us from getting there. From then on it's a matter of planning ways of overcoming the obstacles in our path. The important thing is to keep on doing our present job well. After we've done all the analysis and planning and working, there is still the matter of luck, of being in the right place at the right time, and of other circumstances over which we have no control. How do we deal with this phenomenon? It's easy! We do our planning and we do our job, and then we sit back and let nature take its course. We put our energies into our present job to such an extent that we don't notice the passing of time, the promotions of others, and the missed opportunities. Then we'll be surprised and happy when someone taps us on the shoulder and says, "Congratulations! You're moving on!"

DISCUSSION ACTIVITIES

1. What are some ways of finding out just where we'd like to be going in our career?

2. Discuss (debate) this statement: "Setting a goal really isn't all that important, since the few who ever reach their goal generally change their minds after they get there."

3. Why is self-analysis so difficult for most of us to do?

4. Discuss the merits and demerits of *ambition*.

5. List ways that we can practice and not get better—perhaps even get worse.

6. Discuss (debate) this statement: "In the long run, promotions or moves will more likely be made on the basis of our present performance than on the basis of all the other factors put together."

EPILOGUE

Some kind of award should be given to those who get this far in the book—any book—so that they feel somebody cares. But, alas, there is no award. Perhaps some *rewards*, perhaps even some regrets—at least there is a happy ending. What is it? Why, the knowledge that it is now time to get back to the job and work out your problems without somebody trying to tell you how to do it! That's reward enough for many.

For the experienced supervisor, there is little here that isn't already known (or that couldn't have been figured out with a little contemplation). There is this caution, however. Just to *know* something isn't to *do* something. Just having read all this before, or heard it and studied it in a class somewhere, doesn't make us better supervisors. We have the choice of being just as bad as we've always been (no matter how good we are), or making up our minds to improve and then doing it. Very little that is good in the life of a supervisor is by accident. Before we do things right, we usually have to do quite a bit that's not so good. Perhaps reading this book will remind you of things you used to do well, or bring to your attention things that you are doing improperly. If we've done our part in writing and editing this, we may even have given you some better ways of doing those things you're doing wrong. That should allow us to disappear into the sunset with smiles on our faces. . . .

INDEX

189